Herbert Rowse

TWENTIETH CENTURY ARCHITECTS

Herbert Rowse

Iain Jackson, Simon Pepper and Peter Richmond

Published by Historic England,
The Engine House, Fire Fly Avenue,
Swindon SN2 2EH
www.HistoricEngland.org.uk
Historic England is a Government service championing England's heritage
and giving expert, constructive advice.

© Iain Jackson, Simon Pepper and Peter Richmond

The views expressed in this book are those of the authors and not necessarily
those of Historic England.

First published 2019
ISBN 978-1-84802-549-3 paperback

British Library Cataloguing in Publication data
A CIP catalogue record for this book is available from the British Library.

The right of Iain Jackson, Simon Pepper and Peter Richmond to
be identified as authors of this work has been asserted by them in
accordance with the Copyright, Designs and Patents Act 1988.

All rights reserved
No part of this publication may be reproduced or transmitted in any form or
by any means, electronic or mechanical, including photocopying, recording,
or any information storage or retrieval system, without permission in writing
from the publisher.

Every effort has been made to trace copyright holders and we apologise
in advance for any unintentional omissions, which we would be pleased
to correct in any subsequent edition of this book.

Series editors: Timothy Brittain-Catlin, Barnabas Calder, Elain Harwood
and Alan Powers

Brought to publication by Sarah Enticknap, Publishing, Historic England

Typeset in Quadraat, 10.75pt
Edited by Anne McDowall
Indexed by Sue Vaughan
Page layout by Rod Harrison, Ledgard Jepson Ltd

Printed in the UK by Gomer Press

Front Cover: Birkenhead Woodside ventilation tower

Frontispiece: The Liverpool Philharmonic Hall

Back Cover: Portrait of Herbert J Rowse, circa early 1930s

Contents

	Foreword by Stephen Bayley	vii
	Acknowledgements	ix
	Introduction	xi
1	The early years	1
2	Monumental	13
3	Tunnel structures	43
4	Brick	63
5	Social housing and planning	91
6	Conclusion	111
	Notes	114
	List of works	125
	Further reading	137
	Illustration credits	144
	Index	146

Foreword

Growing-up in Liverpool, it is inevitable that you notice buildings. No other city has such a looming architectural presence; no other city's great achievements and great disgraces are so readily defined by its streetscape and skyline. Long before I knew the word, Liverpool had made me interested in 'design' – by which I mean the power of man-made things to create moods and enhance the ordinary.

From the back seat of my father's Jaguar or Humber, submarine transits of the Mersey through the Tunnel were a regular experience, although not always a good one. I well remember the occasions when, returning from a visit to The Wirral at night, I would be alarmed to see water cascading from the vitreous roof, causing windscreen wipers to be deployed. Of course, I always assumed the river had breached the structure, only to find that cleaning crews were simply washing the tile-work while traffic was light.

Only later did I come to understand that this elaborate and very pleasing tile-work was a happy consequence of the unusually generous bore of the Mersey Tunnel, a civic enterprise like no other. Most tunnels are so claustrophobic, no decorative effects are possible. And it was later still when I learned that the public face of the tunnel, the magnificently confident approach and the ventilation shafts with a presence to rival Lutyens' Cenotaph, were the work of a singular local architect called Herbert Rowse.

And as a teenager, I prowled the streets on architectural tours with a crude single-lens-reflex camera and my copies of Quentin Hughes' *Seaport* and Nikolaus Pevsner's *Pioneers of Modern Design*, the former still the best biography of any city anywhere, the latter the first book to acknowledge Liverpool's place in the modernist story. It was clear even to a 16-year-old that Liverpool's financial district was unique in Europe. When I walk along Water Street today, I think I could be in Wilmington or Baltimore, not Lyon or Verona or any other provincial European city. And it is Herbert Rowse's India Building that creates this utterly distinctive trans-Atlantic feel.

Then there was the Philharmonic Hall, where, in successive months, I attended a talk by Pevsner and a concert by Canned Heat, such was the eclectic culture of Liverpool circa 1969. Of course, now I can talk knowledgeably about how Willem Dudok and the Amsterdam School influenced the design of the Philharmonic, but at the time I simply thought this beautifully proportioned,

The Liverpool Philharmonic Hall

lushly finished and carefully detailed building had a gloriously dignifying effect on anybody who used it – even me in an Afghan coat with a pint of Guinness on board. Of course, it was the work of Herbert Rowse.

Rowse seems to me a very important and impressive figure unjustly neglected, at least until now. Perhaps he was not a truly great architect, but I think he was an exceptional *designer*. His influences were eclectic, but not brainlessly promiscuous. He was not doctrinaire, but nor was he frivolous. He was imaginative and resourceful, but worked to strict personal and professional disciplines. He acknowledged tradition, but was no slavish historicist.

But best of all, Rowse knew the transformative magic that design can perform. He knew about symbolism, details, materials and textures. It mattered to him that buildings *meant* something to the people who pass by them, travel through them and work in them. Rowse's buildings have stories to tell. Thus, his tunnel is more than a tunnel, the India Building more than an office block and the Philharmonic more than a concert hall.

Very simply put: Herbert Rowse sensed the miscegenated glory of Liverpool and gave it unforgettable expression in fine buildings.

STEPHEN BAYLEY

Acknowledgements

We are indebted to the kind help and assistance of so many people who have made this publication possible. We would like to say a special thank you to the Special Collections and Archives at University of Liverpool, especially Jo Klett, Robyn Orr and Sîan Wilks, for their generous and friendly assistance; the University of Liverpool Library, and especially Nicola Kerr, for her infinite patience.

We would also like to thank Nancy Barker, Information Management and Storage, St Helens; Stephen Bayley, Birkenhead Central Library; André Brown; Alun Bull; Valeriea Carullo from RIBA Photographs; Andrew Crompton; Bernard Byrne and Shaun Morrow of Castlewood Property Management Ltd; James Darby of Barclays Group Archives; Ben Duvall; Sarah Enticknap; Jayne Garrity and the Philharmonic Hall; Abigail Garrad; Tom Harker; Elain Harwood; Julian Holder; John Hudson; Roger Hull and Paul Keogh at the Liverpool Record Office; Peter Judge, Group Archives and Museum, Lloyd Banking Group; Anne McDowall; Alan Powers; Mark Rowse; Reg Towner; Siobhan Twomey; Maria White, NSG Group; the staff and archivists at Wirral Archives; The National Archives, Kew; RIBA Library; archivists and staff at the Pharmacy Building at University College London; the owners and residents at Allandale Heswall, Millmead Willaston; and the Woodchurch housing estate.

We are especially grateful to the RIBA Trust Awards, University of Liverpool School of Arts, Liverpool School of Architecture and the Society of Architectural Historians of Great Britain (SAHGB) for generously funding and supporting this project, and for the reviewers' and editors' generous and helpful comments.

Introduction

As the luxury liner *Scythia* docked at Liverpool's Pier Head on Monday 13 December 1926, one of its passengers, Herbert James Rowse, had a perfect view of the city he was about to radically change with his banks, offices, theatre and ventilation towers. No other architect has made such a profound impact on this cityscape and region, with residential, mercantile, cultural and infrastructural projects. Rowse was returning from a month-long fact-finding trip to New York, where he had observed the latest in American construction techniques and methods of integrating building services. The sojourn would inform the detailed design of Martins Bank headquarters following his successful competition win nine months earlier – his largest commission to date, received when he was 39 years of age.

The commission, perhaps more than any other of Rowse's works, was the most complete and polished assembling of form, structure, interior and sculpture. The sheer walls, stretching to nine stories tall, and flat figurative decoration presented something of a different order to what had gone before in the UK. Its innovative massing, structural approach and building services were blended with a restrained classicism scaled to form a city block and applied to a modern office and banking typology. The interior, especially the banking hall, still reveals a luxurious array of materials set within the most generous of proportions and carefully resolved spatial arrangements and sequences. Coupled with Rowse's extraordinary attention to detail, inventive decoration and craftsmanship of the highest order, this is a good-looking, sophisticated building, in the vanguard of a business-responsive and utility-focused, commercial design – albeit one that had reached the zenith of this stylistic approach. It was perhaps the ideal commission for Rowse at that time, offering the chance to incorporate American-inspired design on a steel frame coupled with lavish interiors with eclectic historical references. It would not be fair to view this commission as the pinnacle of his career, because there was much to celebrate prior and afterwards, but it certainly deserves the accolade of being 'probably the best building of its kind in the country'.[1]

Rowse was well prepared for these monumental tasks, having worked on the large Canadian government building in Winnipeg, but like most architects, he began his practice with small domestic projects, preferring to work for himself. He had a personality that found it difficult to comply with instruction or petty office hierarchies and he sought commissions through competition entries.

Aerial view of Liverpool showing Rowse's George's Dock, India Buildings and Martins Bank

In this, he had a mentor and promoter in the form of his old tutor Professor Sir Charles Herbert Reilly. Reilly was a relentless self-publicist and his favourite students received exposure through the professor's writing and contacts. Rowse's career became intricately linked with that of Reilly, and several of Rowse's winning entries were in competitions judged by Reilly. In many ways, this book is also Reilly's story, and, in an extraordinary turn of events, their paths crossed at the end of their careers as the two protagonists become embroiled in the design of a post-war housing-estate controversy.

Rowse achieved early success with his competition wins. His drafting skills and clear articulation of ideas seduced the judging panels, but fundamentally, he sought out clients who were prepared to invest in creating exceptional buildings, designed according to his vision and solution to the brief. Eric Hyde notes that 'small clients who worried about fiddling and false economies were not HJ's [Rowse's] best friends, and he was impatient with those who would not, or could not for financial reasons, think big'.[2] While undoubtedly a skilful artist, he was also a successful businessman, keeping his practice lean, carefully controlled and dedicated to delivering the best quality 'product' possible.

Rowse's work could be considered more curatorial than innovative. This is not meant to be critical or disparaging, for he had an excellent eye for proportion, scale, rhythm and composition, as well as technical skill and close collaborations with excellent masons and sculptors. He learned from the experiments of others, sampling the best from existing precedents and preferring to perfect the craft rather than be a pioneering risk-taker. He had many sourcebooks from which he would draw solutions, particularly for ornamentation. He was courageous in combining a number of precedents from across historical periods, as well as liberally 'citing' other architects whom he admired, and was an avid collector, amassing a significant portfolio of art, furniture, carpets and so on. Throughout his career, he continuously searched for appropriate form. Rarely drawing from something as banal as function, he was eager for his work to express a solid monumentality and a bold, symmetrical stance. This mass of interlocking geometric surfaces was then carefully narrated with sculpture and decorative motifs. There was an underlying classical language to his work (what some have called a modernism with ancestry) but never an orthodox grammar; instead, a search for alternative ornament ensued, often with avant-garde artists bringing the stones alive through their low reliefs, figures, etchings and entablatures. The George's Dock tunnel ventilation shaft, for example, included an array of sculptures depicting themes such as speed and travel through an abstract relief of aviator Amy Johnson, and the continuously open tunnels were represented by the two figures of 'night' and 'day'. The overall composition has some resemblance to ancient Egyptian pylons and the temples at Philae, overlaid with zig-zag decoration and other Art Deco patterns.

St George's Dock Ventilation Tower viewed from the Overhead Railway

Rowse's own interpretation of his work was rare, and he did not engage in self-promotion through lecture tours or publications. He only ever gave three lectures: two at the Liverpool Architectural Society on the opening of Martins Bank and the Mersey Tunnels and the third, 11 years later at Cambridge University, to the Institute of Civil Engineers, where he spoke about the possibility of collaboration between architect and engineer. The latter was an indication of how Rowse saw architecture progressing, through advances in new materials, services and structural possibilities. Only from the 1930s could his work be considered 'modern', but this certainly doesn't detract from its significance; indeed, there is something appealing in Rowse's dogmatic resistance to fashion. Others have tried to excuse Rowse's 'failure' to follow what became an approved modernism, but Rowse stuck to his own methods and principles of solving problems. He was not a conformist or a conservative designer, but neither was he looking for a revolution or making an affected attempt at creating something 'new'.

Rowse realised the value of craft and artisanship, but was equally adept with concrete, steel and glazing, deploying them just as successfully as many so-called modernists. It was the everyday brick, however, that became his core building ingredient. This small, simple, cheap object was used precisely to sculpt exceptional forms, while also making good use of readily available labour and offering protection from the weather and polluted air of Liverpool. If the exterior was frequently an abrupt solid mass of brick built to repel the gritty environment, the interior was the domicile of opulence. The finest materials were sourced and Rowse would design as much of the interior as possible, in some cases down to the carpets, door handles and furniture. He also recognised the role of sculptors and artisans in enhancing his work and left considerable room for collaboration, working closely with an expert ensemble of stone masons, decorators and sculptors.

1 The early years

Rowse was born in Crosby, a small coastal town north of Liverpool, but spent considerable time moving around the North of England as his father's construction business demanded. At the age of 16, he was articled to Liverpool architects Richard Owens and Son,[1] before enrolling at University of Liverpool School of Architecture two years later in 1905.

The School offered a variety of day and evening courses, and in 1902, the two-year Certificate in Architecture course gained exemption from the RIBA Intermediate Examination, as well as a 12-month reduction in the period of articled pupillage by Liverpool architects.[2] Rowse entered the profession via this route, and subsequently received a somewhat shorter formal education than the students who followed (a full-time day course was made available only in 1906). This was a transitional period for the profession as it moved away from the articled system towards a formal university education.

Reilly and the School of Architecture

The School was led by the charismatic, somewhat controversial figure of Professor Charles Herbert Reilly (1874–1948), who had just taken up his position and begun a significant and radical transformation of its studio curriculum.[3] The School's collection of gothic casts and models were replaced with classical ornaments, and a renewed interest was kindled in the Greek–Roman revival architecture of Liverpool, so vividly demonstrated by the likes of Harvey Elmes, Charles Cockerell and John Foster, Junior. The buildings designed by these pioneers were surveyed and then depicted by the students in fastidious measured drawings, and eventually published in the *Portfolio of Measured Drawings*, as Reilly notes:

> I am convinced that there is no better exercise for the student of architecture than in the dissection and reconstruction of the work of the masters, by careful and complete measurements taken on the spot from the buildings themselves. Only so does every subtlety in the design become apparent as the mind of the original artist gradually unfolds itself to that of the student.[4]

Despite the brevity of his course, and Reilly's concern that 'the office-bred student' would have to eradicate a 'narrow outlook, and the bad methods of design and drawing',[5] Rowse wasted no time in honing his drawing skills.

Perspective drawing of Palazzo della Gran Guardia

No doubt his family background in construction bolstered his technical ability. While most other students were content to survey the buildings of Liverpool, Rowse made a pilgrimage to Wren's Greenwich Hospital, perfecting his renderings, washes and drafts,[6] before being awarded the prestigious Holt Travelling Scholarship in 1907.[7] In light of the School's direction, it was predictable that Rowse chose to visit Italy, where he surveyed the Palazzo Pompeii and Palazzo della Gran Guardia, in Verona. The drawing style of the School was somewhat anti-picturesque, and heavily indebted to the Ecole des Beaux-Arts approach of strong ceremonial classical vistas depicted through precise rendered drawings. Rowse was awarded second place in the RIBA Silver Medal for the Verona drawings, although Reilly bemoaned the fact that they 'were before their time in being most magnificently rendered at a time when few people in England could cast a shadow correctly,' and claimed that they would have been placed first a few years later.[8]

Closer to home, the model village of Port Sunlight was also being planned at this time, and Reilly designed a row of terraced cottages for the village. Reilly's work stands out in Port Sunlight for its attempts to introduce an urbane, Regency-inspired terrace, more reminiscent of Brighton than a Cheshire town. The same brief was set for the students, and one of Rowse's first design projects was to design a cottage for the model village.

In many ways, these two student projects are illustrative of the schemes and problems that Rowse tackled throughout his career – those of the monumental structure and the dwelling. The monumental project offers the chance to operate at an urban, if not city scale, and holds many attractions for ambitious architects eager to make an impression, but so too does the house. This most fundamental, rudimentary, yet incredibly difficult design problem is a challenge for all architects, especially when it is to imbue a sense of community and be constructed economically. From one-off villas and semi-detached company houses through to low-rise flats and housing estates, Rowse was very concerned with the problem of housing in all of its forms and scales.

During the first five years of his tenure, Reilly also courted the interest of Port Sunlight's sponsor, the soap magnate and architectural enthusiast William Hesketh Lever (later Lord Leverhulme). It was this relationship that led, in 1909, to Lever funding the creation of the Civic Design School and the *Town Planning Review*, as well as the migration of the School from Alfred Waterhouse's gothic tower to the 'Queen-Anne' Blue Coat School in the city centre – surely a metaphor for the architectural spirit that Reilly was pursuing.[9] Rowse would have been fully exposed to this evolution of the School, and the sense of enthusiasm, energy and entrepreneurship that Reilly exuded. The School's keen interest in classical architecture was blended with an American-inflected Beaux Arts planning, and both Reilly and Rowse looked towards America and the steel-framed 'classical movement' taking place there.[10]

THE EARLY YEARS

Elevation drawing of Palazzo della Gran Guardia

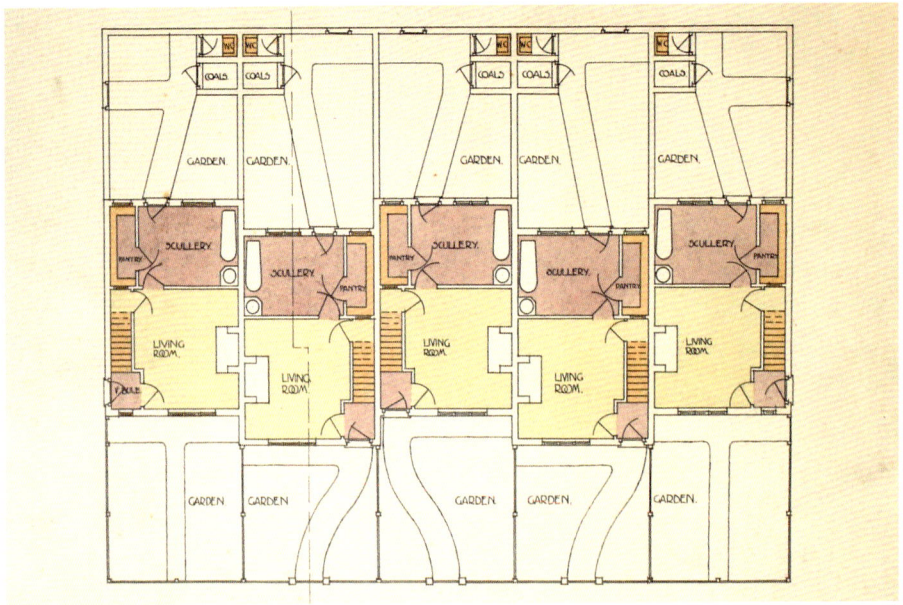

Student project for Port Sunlight cottages

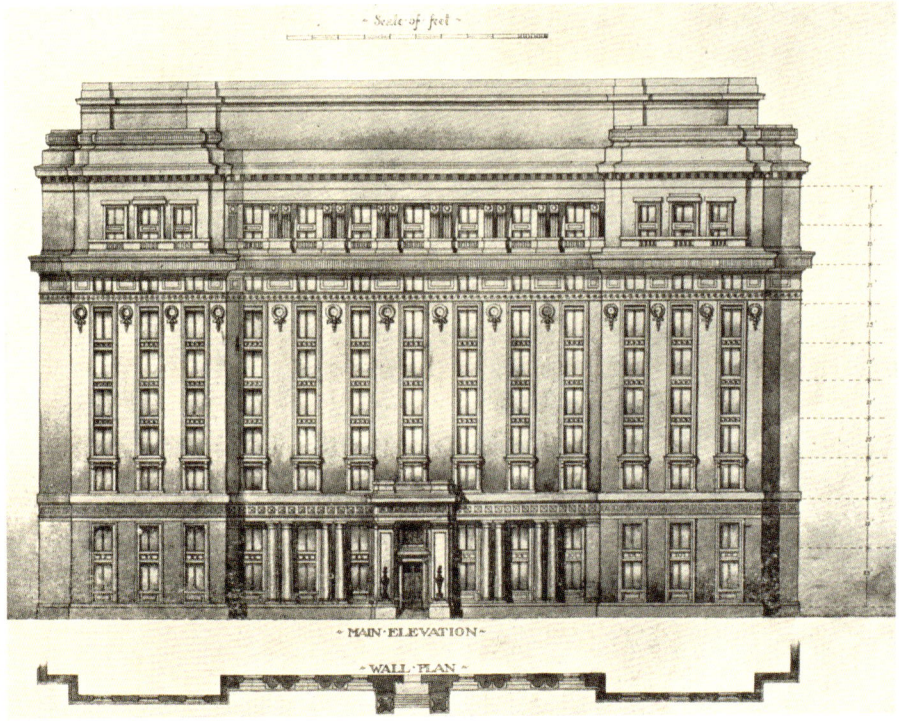

E C Preston's student project, revealing American influences

Their ambition to witness for themselves the creation of the American city was not immediately fulfilled, but after stirring Lever's curiosity, and gaining access to his funding, Reilly first visited America in 1909. He returned loaded with drawings and publications, and by 1911, distinct American flavours were rippling through the studio, as shown in E C Preston's office block, which included upper-storey step-backs, rusticated base, plain mid-section and decorated attic and upper floors.[11]

Looking to America

While Renaissance Italian architecture was a major precedent for Rowse's early development and studies, it was his experience in America that transformed his approach and presented new modes of composing façades, decoration and structural techniques. It also exposed him to the latest modes of heating and ventilation, building services and management, as well as the business of building and the notion of real estate. As a young and fledgling architect, commissions to create such structures in the UK eluded him at that time, but he managed to secure employment with the Beaux-Arts-trained Frank Simon (1862–1933)[12] and gained associate RIBA membership in 1910. During his studies, Rowse would have observed the construction of some of Simon's buildings, especially the Liverpool Cotton Exchange, a triumphantly Edwardian Baroque palace with an interior that surely influenced Rowse's later work on Water Street.

Simon's competition-winning success continued, and he was awarded the Winnipeg Manitoba Parliament project in 1912. Rowse was employed to assist, although he also had competition successes of his own with the Coventry Municipal Buildings in 1911 (third premium), and a housing estate in Prestatyn the following year. Fulfilling his ambition to visit North America, Rowse arrived in Quebec, Canada on 14 June 1912, having sailed from Liverpool. He travelled with both of his parents and perhaps there was an intention for the family to pursue business there.[13] It was not a prolonged visit, however, as Rowse remade the week-long journey from Liverpool just a few months later in December 1912, this time remaining in North America for one year.[14]

Rowse's final destination was listed as Winnipeg, where he joined Simon to work on site at the grandiose Parliament building. This all too familiar symmetrical 'set piece', arranged around perpendicular axes, would have offered little challenge to Rowse, but it was the experience of managing a large site that he sought, further fuelling his craving for a substantial commission of his own. Once the working drawings were completed, Rowse began 'a tour of architectural adventure' and, according to Reilly, worked his way through Canada and the US 'staying in one office after another till he had accumulated enough funds to move on'.[15] Reilly subsequently adopted this idea of an American pilgrimage and period of work experience as a teaching tool, and he arranged

Elevation of Winnipeg Manitoba Parliament

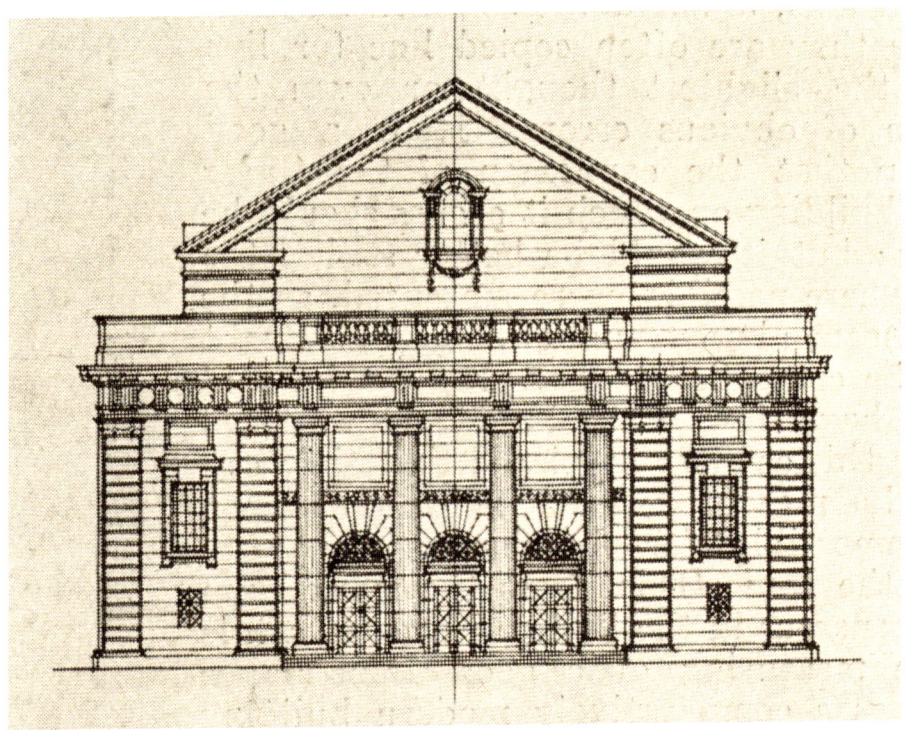

Elevation of Coventry Municipal Buildings competition entry

summer-vacation placements for his students in the US.[16] After a brief period back in the UK in December 1913, Rowse returned the following spring to Winnipeg via New York.[17] He visited the works of McKim, Mead and White so beloved by Reilly, as well as purchasing a substantial folio of American architectural competition submissions.[18] The book was a trove of the latest work to be produced in the States, and included all placed entries as well as the winning schemes; it became Rowse's sourcebook for future commissions. This latest American sojourn was cut short, however, following the outbreak of World War I, and he returned to Liverpool in June 1914, where he worked for the Admiralty on a variety of war-effort structures.[19]

Early house projects

Sir Robert Lowdon Connell, a shipowner and friend of the Rowse family, commissioned a timber conservatory extension (with rather dainty Doric columns) at Blundellsands. The work was similar to that of his student contemporaries also nurturing fledgling practices and cutting their teeth on small residential projects. Lionel Budden and J Ernest Marshall's houses in the Wirral were of a similar type, as was Harold Dod's work in Mossley Hill, and slightly later, Edwin Maxwell Fry's work at Virginia Water.[20]

Conservatory at Blundellsands

Other early commissions came from friends and family and included a small detached brick house for his mother on a remote three-acre plot close to the village of Willaston, Wirral. High-quality materials and precise construction were coupled with an efficient, humble interior, arranged to catch the sun and overlook the garden. Rowse married Dorothy Parry in 1918 and received a commission from his wife's uncle to design Allandale in Heswall, where the Rowses were also living.[21] Both Allandale and his mother's house have neo-Georgian undertones but are horizontal in emphasis, more aligned to a country residence than a town house.

Millmead House, Willaston, 1921

THE EARLY YEARS

Allandale, Heswall, 1921 (photo taken in 2016)

It was part of a burgeoning growth of individually commissioned housing on West Wirral, being close enough to commute to Liverpool via train, ferry and soon via motor car through the Mersey Tunnel. The houses are restrained and somewhat cautious attempts, with little spatial extravagance, apart from the staircases being carefully framed by Doric pilasters and complemented by delicate handrails. If the houses were structurally and aesthetically guarded, they were more adventurous in their servicing, and included integrated gadgets such as automatic vacuum cleaners concealed within the skirting boards. Rowse's early concern for labour-saving devices and carefully hidden services reflected not only the shifts in the social structures of the time, but also a kind of modernity that has received far less interest than the bold, if somewhat stylistic, preoccupations of the architectural press.

Rowse was not afraid to pursue a different approach, however, and at Garthlands in Heswall he opted for a more radical choice of material and construction than his earlier brick residences, employing concrete as the main structural and façade material, with advice given by his 'concrete engineer' younger brother.[22] The house is of a much larger scale and more elaborately decorated than the earlier brick dwellings, and the choice of concrete illustrates a desire to develop new techniques and solutions to housing production. He was also responding to broader debates within the construction industry around standardisation, wet trades and building efficiency.[23] It was an experiment Rowse would not repeat, and concrete remained unexposed on all future projects.

Garthlands (concrete house), Heswall, 1924

THE EARLY YEARS

Rowse returned to a stuccoed conventional villa for Heswall Golf Club, with a bold loggia running across the west-facing façade providing shelter and views out over the course and estuary beyond. The small groined vaults provided the test cases for much larger work that was to follow at Martins Bank.[24] The commission was awarded following a fire that destroyed the old club, and Reilly was employed to adjudicate the architectural competition. Rowse (who was a member of the club and living close by) was picked out, and Reilly received his 20 guineas fee, setting a precedent that would repeat itself on several future occasions. Competition success continued with first place (with Lionel Budden[25]) on the unbuilt King's College Library, Cambridge in 1924; and most importantly the India Buildings, in collaboration with Arnold Thornley (1870–1953).

Heswall Golf Club, proposed façade, 1925

2 Monumental

We have determined that Monumental Architecture shall be the basis of our system.[1]

The leanness and frustration of the war years were slowly countered by a growing confidence in the city as the anticipation of peace grew, and Rowse was fully prepared, having maintained a small office at No. 9 Cook Street in Liverpool. His first major commission came from the sugar trade, one of the largest industries in the city. Maxwell Fry recalled how 'The smell of molasses came in pungent waves up the slopes from the docks into the financial centre' and business men in top hats 'and hands deep in trouser pockets talked money as they walked from one set of chambers to another'.[2] Liverpool handled over 40 per cent of the UK's sugar imports and processing, plus associated industries such as jam and confectionary, and re-establishing trade after World War I was paramount. On the 'Tuesday following Armistice', Rowse received a £40,000 commission to design a refinery for Manbré and Garton.[3] At first glance, Manbré and Garton appears as any other functional daylight factory, with its extensive glazed façade set within a grid of masonry. But it is here that we start to see a concern for hierarchy, an inventive layering of decorative elements and the use of a monochrome material laid in a variety of ways to highlight entrances, generate vertical emphasis on the 'book-end' elements, and proud or recessed coursing to express different components of the façade. Bricks were laid vertically to form capitals, cornices and plinths. The refinery was elevated as an object of praise, before such notions of 'architectural machines' were receiving such popular reception, and was designed with unusual attention to detail for this type of building. It was a celebration of the factory and a pageant of brickwork detailing.

These projects enabled Rowse to firmly establish his practice, but he was eager for more prestigious challenges, and set about entering the most prominent architectural competitions of the day. This resulted in two of his largest and perhaps most important buildings in Liverpool – Martins Bank and India Buildings. Located on either side of Water Street, one of Liverpool's seven ancient streets, these two palaces sit adjacent to the Town Hall, almost undermining it as the real seats of power in the city. They represent the two business empires that made Liverpool: banking, generating capital for trade and speculation, and shipping, the art of long-distance logistics and the means by which the UK could export its manufactured goods. Neither 'industry' *made* anything –

The Manbré and Garton sugar refinery, Liverpool 1918

rather they both facilitated business and the ability to transfer finance and goods. It is of little surprise that, along with the 'Three Graces' at Pier Head, these two buildings are of exceptional magnitude and extravagance.

India Buildings

After World War I and the sudden economic boom that followed, Alfred Holt & Co, the owners of the Blue Funnel Line, began orchestrating a new development to reflect the prestige of their growing business. They were eager to keep up with their main rivals Cunard, who in 1917, had completed their new offices on the Pier Head site to the designs of Willink and Thicknesse, and the White Star Line's distinctive 'bacon-rasher' building by Norman Shaw.

Holts saw an opportunity to divert their 'enormous profits' from the early 1920s into property development, diversifying their business portfolio.[4] They began to systematically acquire the smaller properties adjacent to their headquarters at India Buildings, establishing a significant portfolio in the heart of the city covering an entire block. Working with architect-surveyor Edmund Kirby, they proposed to widen the streets surrounding the block by demolishing all of the acquired buildings and reducing the overall building-plot size. It was a move that also suited the municipality and enabled a stronger urban form to emerge from the hotchpotch 19th-century efforts. The increased road

The Old India Buildings, Liverpool

widths were not merely a civic gesture, but also permitted the new structure to be built to a greater height without infringing on the neighbouring 'right to light'. It was the 'right to light' argument that determined the overall height of India Buildings, with a line drawn at 67 degrees from the ground-floor windowsill of the building on the opposite side of the street to the site boundary of India Buildings.[5] Once all 23 buildings were acquired and settlements paid to neighbouring buildings, the project was to be constructed in two phases, with Holts remaining operational in the old India Buildings that occupied half of the plot. Upon completion of the first phase, the businesses and tenants would migrate into the new building to allow phase two to commence.

A limited architectural competition was held to decide on the final scheme, and Arnold Thornley and Frank Gatley Briggs (1862–1921) were invited to submit a proposal. They were an ideal choice, having already designed the flamboyant Mersey Docks and Harbour Board Offices (1907), and had recently completed Wallasey Town Hall as well as the Bank of British West Africa, a building much praised by Reilly.[6] The practice workload, coupled with Briggs' untimely death, prompted Thornley to seek a new collaborator for the competition, and he invited Rowse to join him.[7] Rowse very much took the lead on the design and, according to Reilly, 'it was for this competition that Rowse first collected a team of young men to work with him at his house in Heswall' to prepare the drawings.[8]

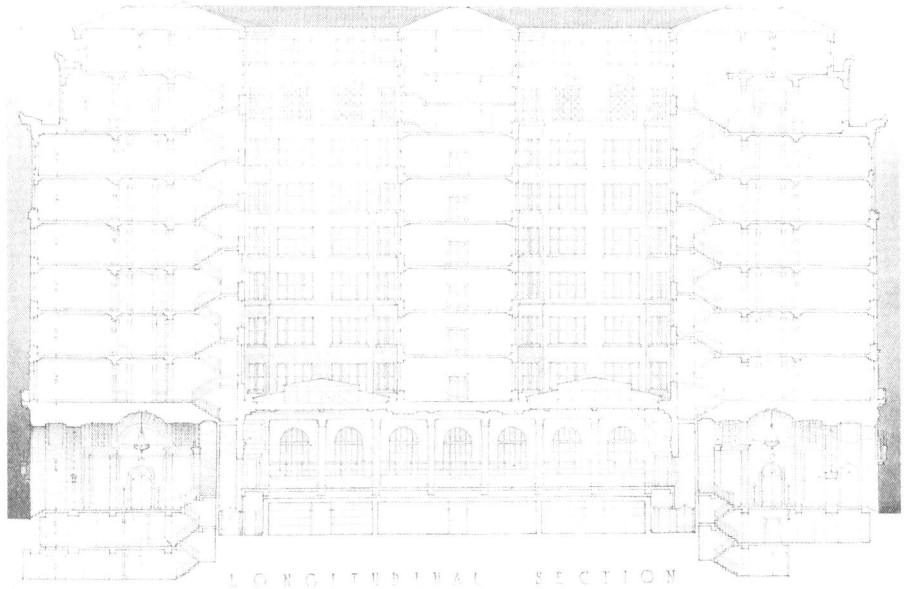

Competition drawing for India Buildings: section

Competition drawing for India Buildings: elevation

Competition drawings for India Buildings: elevation to Water Street

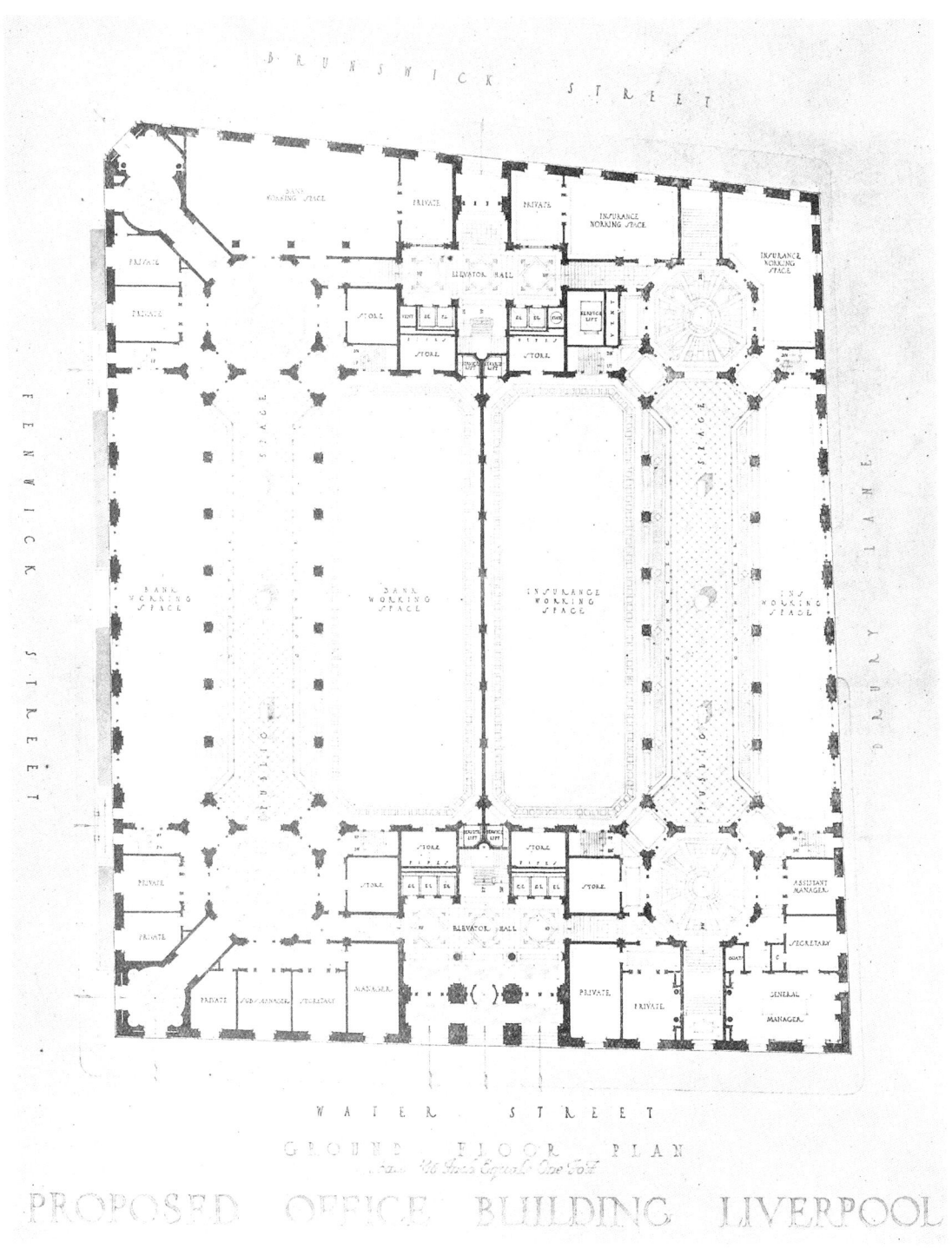

Competition drawings for India Buildings: ground-floor plan

Rowse proposed a grand ground-floor ceiling height of seven metres, which was also reflected on the rusticated exterior base, the vast expanse of wall dispersed with rounded arched openings and clerestory windows above. The mid-portion of the building is composed of a plain grid of Portland stone punched with square windows, before the restrained decoration of the attic stories and large projecting cornice. It was rational, precise and abrupt, with only the slightest flicker of emotion expressed from the Juliet balconies and keystone scrolls. *The Liverpolitan* noted, 'Straight and sheer, strong and clearly stamped against the sky, it tells a story of its own. It leaves the old age behind and looks gloriously to the new age … a business vortex and the India Buildings stands firm in the centre.'[9]

Reilly compared the building to the best examples from New York as well as others within Liverpool: 'The West African Bank, the Cunard Building, the Adelphi Hotel, are all buildings of simple rectangular shape relying for effect not on an array of columns or other trappings, but on the fine articulation of the strength their mass gives them.'[10]

India Buildings, Water Street, showing the 7m-high ground-floor rusticated base

Occupying a plot size of 82 × 70m, it was a vast undertaking and described by *The Liverpolitan* as a 'self-contained town'.[11] Indeed, it was soon to become a thriving hive occupied by 2,000 office workers, with more found in the shops, tailors, tobacconists, chemists and confectioners on its ground floor. A Constitutional Club was based there with around 800 members. For managers arriving by car, an on-site mechanic was on hand for repairs and maintenance, and for those travelling via train, there was a direct tunnel to James Street Station. *The Liverpolitan* further listed the array of activities: 'Dances and concerts, exhibitions, whist drives, examinations, receptions, conferences are held there. To suites of offices high above a fleet of ten lifts is all day rising and hovering. The vast and complicated network of His Majesty's telephones in Liverpool is directed here. The Inland Revenue is also to be found among the ten floors.'[12]

Consisting of a steel frame with Portland stone walls and Italian Renaissance detailing, it occupies an entire city block and rises nine storeys. The combination of functions within the building, housing as it does office accommodation along with a bank, post office, shops and an underground station, set it apart from previous commercial developments in the city. It was the first of the large Liverpool office buildings inspired by early 20th-century American commercial building in the Beaux-Arts manner. Construction costs were £1.25 million, and this large sum is reflected in the highest quality of material and finish used throughout the building. The arched entrances on Water Street and Brunswick Street open onto vaulted travertine-lined elevator halls, which are in turn linked by a tunnel-vaulted arcade of shops running through the centre of the building. The arcade – not a part of the original scheme – is also travertine lined, and the individual shop fronts have elegant bronze-framed detailing. Corner entrances to the north-east and south-east lead to polygonal lobbies. The exterior is embellished with sculptural carving by Edmund C Thompson. Above the main Water Street entrance, below the level of the top floor windows and set into a meander-pattern frieze that completely enfolds the building, is a crest carved with a figure of Neptune kneeling in a scallop shell supported by two reclining Tritons, reflecting the owner's maritime commercial interests.

The project engulfed the former Chorley Street, which was incorporated into the project post-competition as a shopping arcade cutting through the centre of the building, its vaulted entrances receiving only scant decoration from sculptor Edmund C Thompson.[13] The bronze lamps on either side of the entrance were made by the Bromsgrove Guild and modelled closely on the Palazzo Strozzi, Florence. The arcade invokes the central alley that was mandatory in the design of Chicago offices that India Buildings was clearly indebted to. The seventh floor replicated the arrangement of Holts's old offices, with its 'open-plan "quarter-deck", so preserving the Holts tradition of a management accessible to one another, and in touch with other staff'.[14]

India Buildings: arcade ceiling vaults

The competition brief stated that the two halves of the ground floor were to be let to large businesses, such as an insurance company and a bank. Ten passenger lifts served the ten storeys, stretching to 36m at the main parapet and 45m overall. The sloping site and construction sequencing meant that the ground floor was raised half a storey, providing some light into the basement while accommodating the connecting tunnel to James Street underground station. Lightwells brought daylight into the deep plan, but they were not seen as utilitarian courtyards: not one service pipe or conduit is exposed. Rowse attended a talk at the RIBA on the latest American building methods by Harvey Corbett (the architect of Bush House, London), but judging by his question to the speaker, he was expecting a more thorough examination of services and mechanical installations than the somewhat rudimentary introduction to 'setbacks' and steel-framed structures.[15]

The competition also resulted in the consolidation of Rowse's practice. His office was kept deliberately compact, with a group of hard-working assistants kept under close control. Arthur Scarlett joined Rowse from Thornley's practice after the India Buildings competition, and Donald Bradshaw also joined after

India Buildings: Lloyds bank interior on the ground floor

designing the interior furniture and fittings for India Buildings. According to Eric Hyde, Rowse was the 'strong, dynamic, exuberant, artist technician and provided the inspiration for the design ... Bradshaw a devoted chief designer [who could] interpret Rowse's ideas; and Scarlett, the contracts expert who oversaw constructional detailing and carefully saw that everything went together as intended'.[16] This trinity employed only another four or so assistants, thereby maintaining considerable control of the design and detailing as well as keeping office expenses to a minimum. Rowse also wove into his design and fee schedule additional office space for his practice to occupy on completion. For the clients, this was largely inconsequential in light of the overall office space they were procuring, but it offered Rowse the chance not only to curtail his overheads but also to occupy prestigious offices that could be used as an advertisement and showcase for his own work. He relocated the practice to India Buildings, and later, when Martins Bank was completed, his practice moved into that building on the same terms. He also secured a similar arrangement with the Mersey Tunnels, gaining a 'free pass' through the toll booths. These may seem like petty arrangements, but they are indicative of how Rowse ran his business.

Rowse's office in Martins Bank

Rowse's drawing office in Martins Bank

Martins Bank

The late 1920s and early 1930s was a period of great activity in bank building, as many firms merged and subsequent reorganisation prompted the construction of purpose-built premises.[17] There were around 12 banks in the Castle Street area of the city, including the aforementioned Bank of West Africa, and the Bank of England branch by Charles Robert Cockerell. There was a rich classical tradition expressed in these works with the desire to, 'impress the public with the dignity, solidity and reliability of their institutions',[18] and Rowse studied these types carefully. By 1 March 1926, the competition designs for a new Martins Bank headquarters had been anonymously submitted from a select field of four London- and four Liverpool-based architects – with the schemes again judged by Reilly.[19] The Liverpool-based firms included Arnold Thornley, Rowse's former collaborator on the India Buildings; his former classmate Harold Dod (collaborating with Willink), who had just completed the Liverpool Athenaeum Club; and the prolific architect–surveyors Edmund Kirby, who were responsible for negotiating the land/light and property disputes surrounding the site acquisition. It was eager competition to say the least. Reilly gave the award to the plans labelled 'number 4', and 'on the sealed envelope being opened it was found that Mr Herbert Rowse was the successful competitor.'[20]

Martins wanted a banking hall that reflected their stature and ambition, as well as offices and directors' suites, but of equal importance was maximising the amount of lettable office space on the intermediate floors. It was a similar business model to India Buildings, but with a more complex set of programmes and a smaller site. Despite these limitations, the solution was more refined: all details were fully resolved, and any planning compromises that had emerged in the India Buildings were eliminated here.[21] The result may be considered Rowse's masterpiece.

Occupying an irregular rectilinear site of 43 × 55m and rising to 46m tall, Martins Bank contains 10 storeys above ground with a further two below. A series of colonnades on the roof crown the edifice and neatly connect the protruding plant-rooms, water-tanks and Manager's penthouse, as well as framing exquisite views over the city, river and distant Welsh mountains. The decoration is 'judiciously concentrated at the top and bottom' of the building, with greater emphasis 'placed on the beauty of proportion than on surface decoration'.[22] It does have a very flat, almost sheer finish, a look that would have been even more startling had the Bank not insisted on increasing the size of the windows.[23] Rowse had originally proposed a façade with only slender openings to counter the thin veneer of stone and to stress the building's mass and sense of fortress-like solidity. The Bank's directors were very much involved in the design development, and Rowse made several changes to his design to accommodate their requests and ideas.[24]

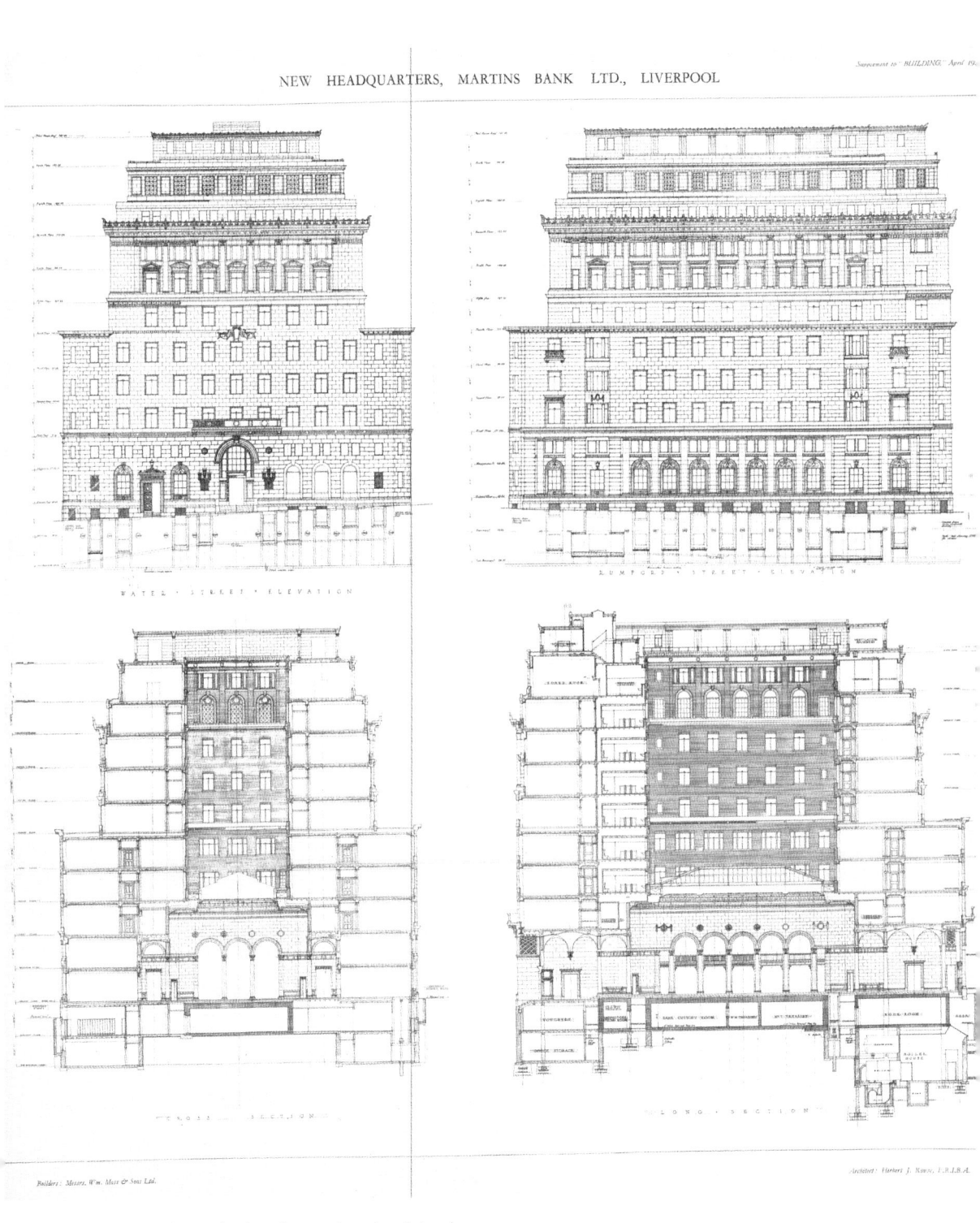

Martins Bank: elevations and sectional drawings

Martins Bank and Liverpool Town Hall

Also, they did not employ a 'main contractor' to manage and arrange the subcontractors, but instead organised tenders directly from each of the various trades and fabricators, thus ensuring that they not only obtained the best prices but also retained complete control over the construction process and quality. It was a time-consuming and highly supervisory approach, but one that Rowse was very happy to engage with.[25]

There were a number of design problems that Rowse had to address in this scheme. Principally, he needed to provide a large and open banking hall on the ground floor with the central teller counter visually uninterrupted and well-lit. This was the main publicly accessible room and face of the business. The deep site prompted a central lighting well, which brought light down to the banking hall's glazed roof. The challenge was to then fit as much office space into the intermediate floors not required by the bank. Circular corner lobbies to the south-west and north-east provide access to rentable office accommodation on the upper storeys. The singular lettable office space formed the modular unit around which the intermediate floor plates were designed. The office unit was then duplicated in double-bank formation around a 'hollow-square plan', which would allow daylight into the inner ring of offices.

Martins Bank viewed from India Buildings

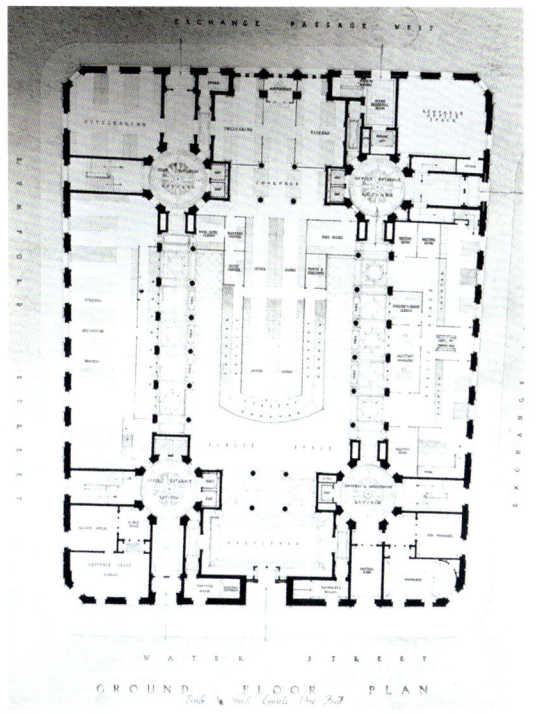

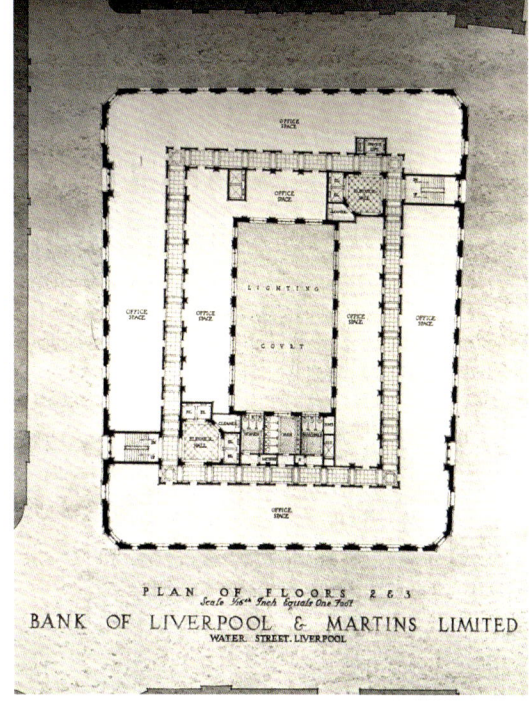

Competition drawings for Martins Bank: ground-floor plan

Competition drawings: second- and third-floor plan

It was a well-tested model, as found at the Rand-McNally and the Rookery Building, Chicago, both of which were on similarly sized plots. The plans of the Illinois Merchants Bank (1924), Builders Building (1927), Railway Exchange (1915) and Peoples Gas Company Building (1911) also display a very similar floor plan and were proven examples of successful commercial offices that would have been well known to Rowse. The sheer walls of the Chicago model, with its stringent pre-1920s building codes, were coupled with references to New York 'set-backs' to create a strong image that mirrored the latest efforts of corporate America, and the high-yielding returns these buildings could muster would have been familiar to Martins, who were eager to emulate the same business model.[26]

In order to fit the double-banked offices around a central corridor, Rowse had to cantilever them out above the banking hall below. Without the cantilever, he would have had to reduce the size either of the office spaces (thereby making the development less profitable) or the hall, or introduce a series of columns within the hall – none of which was appropriate or attractive.[27] It was this use of the steel frame and the somewhat daring approach of cantilevering eight stories of office space that solved the design conundrum.

CROSS SECTION
Scale 1/16 Inch Equals One Foot

Competition drawings showing the cantilever above the banking hall

Martins Bank under construction, viewed from Town Hall

Martins Bank under construction, viewed from Water Street

It went to the very limits of what was technically possible, and the frame began to show some deflection during construction as the upper floors were added, prompting additional reinforcement and deepening of the cantilever beam to take the strain.

Reilly acknowledged that 'it was this use of steel construction which I think more than anything else won him the competition',[28] confessing that 'some of us older ones might have been a little chary' of such a move.[29] Although Reilly was again the common denominator in Rowse being awarded yet another commission, it is unlikely that he could have swayed the client had the building not also demonstrated this strong commercial promise.[30] While the creative structural gymnastics were at the forefront of modern construction, the steel frame was not 'expressed' but was encased in concrete and faced with a Portland-stone ashlar rainscreen, giving the impression of a solid, load-bearing façade. The cantilever remains discreet too, almost concealed, as if it were tectonic cheating. The interior steel columns were also enveloped with monolithic hunks of cylindrical Travertine marble, bored out from end to end and then threaded in one piece onto the structure 'to give the effect of a solid marble column'.[31] It was an extraordinary approach to maintain the illusion of a functioning column, and the only suitable method to avoid unsightly joints and clashes in the marble grain. Each column had to be carefully wrapped and protected against future knocks and damage during the rest of the building work.[32]

Rowse's solution at ground-floor level avoided any compromise, and additional floors could then be added to create more office spaces, but only up to a certain level, as dictated by ancient light rights claimed by neighbouring buildings.

Cantilevered steel frame of Martins Bank under construction

The response was to set back the upper stories, again making full use of the structural properties of steel-frame construction, while also generating a strong geometric form, with restrained decoration derived from 'Florentine prototypes'.[33] Rowse also used steel cantilevers to support the large projecting cornices. This eliminated the requirement for a large counterweight parapet to hold the cornices in place, which would have interrupted the fenestration pattern and involved additional expense.

Reilly bemoaned the fact that the Bank was not in the 'modernist' manner (quickly forgetting his own volte-face and that he was co-designing a similar building in London at the same time) but acknowledged that the Bank and India Buildings were 'extraordinarily modern in all their arrangements'.[34] Writing for *The Banker*, Reilly again espoused the structural advances:

> It is a style born, among other things, of steel construction, the desire to give expression to mass rather than to detail, and the need for economy of labour and materials, to the multiple use of buildings, whether as blocks of flats or of offices. Its general characteristic may be said to be its starkness, its grim truthfulness to the new needs and the new construction which have brought it into being. Starkness, however, is no bad quality in architecture.[35]

The exterior does have a blunt seriousness (perhaps less so than India Buildings), but the same cannot be said for the interior. Reilly noted how the banking hall was 'the essential feature of the American bank. Other departments to which the public as a whole have not access may be hidden away on other stories, but the hall is the centre of activity, the kernel of the building. Nothing is allowed to interfere with its dignity or to mar its proportions.'[36] Rowse followed this approach, making the hall a lofty two storeys tall with an intermediate mezzanine providing additional banking offices. It was modelled closely on the National City Bank in New York by McKim, Mead and White. Reilly had also featured this project in his monograph on the firm in 1924, its vaulting and centralised teller counter setting a clear precedent for Rowse to follow.[37] Rowse having explained to the Building Committee that Holts had used travertine marble extensively throughout India Buildings, the Committee instructed him to order the finest quality marbles. Rowse opted to clad the peninsula counter with purple Levatine, Verde Antico and black marbles, contrasting with the cream of the travertine used on the columns and entrance vestibules. He also designed steel fireproof furniture so that the banking books did not have to be returned to the vaults every evening, saving hours of work and improving security. Other time- and labour-saving devices included a conveyor belt to carry cheques around the teller bench (inspired by the sugar-factory commissions), rather than them having to be collected by clerks, and 'safety beams' that prevented the lift doors from closing on passengers, rendering attendants superfluous.

Horseshoe teller counter

Interior of Martins Bank: lift lobby

The building's structural grid of 3.5m (11'6") also informed the service layouts, with thermostats in each room controlling low-temperature ceiling heating panels. The Building Committee and Rowse visited a number of buildings in London, including Bush House, to see similar heating solutions, eager to ensure their cutting-edge solutions were up to the task.[38] A series of vertical ducts enabled electrical power, lighting and telephone cables to be distributed and maintained, while horizontal ducts dispensed services to the various office arrangements, eliminating the need for surface-mounted cables, pipes and associated expensive alterations with each new tenant.[39] The obsession with detail even extended to the lighting in the toilets, with switching triggered by the closing of the cubicle door. The delicate, almost frameless, steel windows are openable, but the main ventilation was provided by an air-handling unit that filtered and warmed the air as required and, unlike an open window, dampened external noise. The prepared air was then piped around the building, entering the offices via specially designed outlets decorated with a pyramidal stack of coins. An electricity substation was housed in the basement, along with the oil-fired boilers and the most intriguing and protected room in all banks: the vault, hermetically sealed to preserve interned documents and containing an alarm system in case an operative got accidently locked inside.[40]

If the plan, façade and banking hall were overtly American in influence, the ornamentation and other interior spaces looked to Europe. Rowse had a large collection of source books that he mined for ideas and solutions, often blending a number of styles and periods. The directors' board room, located on the eighth floor, was given special decorative treatment: an eclectic mix of medievalism and Renaissance Palace with Egyptian touches combining to provide an extremely fine example of an Art Deco interior. As well as a carpet designed by Rowse, there is a marble fireplace that invokes the 17th-century dining room at the Marquise de Los Alamos's house, Jerez, Spain. This was placed beneath the beamed walnut ceiling, carved into ornate geometric patterns derived from the 15th-century throne room of the Aljafería Palace, a fortified medieval Islamic palace in Zaragoza, Spain.[41]

Was there an overt symbolic reference being deployed in using the counting house of an Islamic caliphate and the dining hall of aristocrats? Was Rowse attempting to create a sense of history, longevity, pedigree and governance? And if so, why was he sampling from Southern Europe? There is a sense that he wanted to modulate the bald exterior with something more energetic and startling for the hallowed interior preserve of the directors. He was also eager to source alternative forms of decoration from outside the Greco-Roman lexicon, eagerly borrowing from a broad range of traditions. The tunnel extract towers, for example (as briefly mentioned in the introduction), include imaginary Ancient Egyptian motifs, perhaps responding to the recent discovery of Tutankhamun's tomb, and here within the Bank, there was a desire to invent,

Fireplace, Marquise de Los Alamos's house, Jerez, Spain

Director's board room fireplace in Martins Bank

Aljafería Palace ceiling, Zaragoza, Spain

or re-imagine, a regal dynasty that would supply a range of patterns and themes for Rowse to apply. It is a curious composition, but the careful arrangement, proportions and fine materials all seem to perfectly nestle and create a refined and contemplative retreat from the bustle of the banking hall below.

Other decoration was less cryptic, and inspired by nautical themes, as found at Mersey Docks and Harbour Board Building (such as crabs, lobsters and mermaids), as well as references to finance (including Midas, stacks of coins and money bags) and the role Liverpool played in the Atlantic slave trade (two African boys holding bags of money). The grasshopper and liver bird motif also feature as symbols of the Bank's heritage and merger between Martins and the Bank of Liverpool in 1918.[42] Herbert Tyson Smith carved most of the stone decoration, and brought much 'wit, nuances, and detail' that enlivened the elevations initially drawn by Rowse.[43] More than 40 sculptors worked under Smith's direction, such was the scale and extent of the embellishment.

Director's ceiling in Martins Bank

Thomas Shaw and George Capstick were also among the artisans employed and they would go on to contribute to the Mersey Tunnel entrances.[44] While it is possible to discern the individual strands of Rowse's influences and his liberal use of existing precedents, it was his ability to assimilate and blend them into a meaningful composition that reveals his remarkable skill. He was resolving a complex site, providing solutions to the contradictory requirements of real estate and branding, and integrating the most modern of structural solutions and building services. This was all coupled with references to historical European design and the latest trends from a suave corporate America.

Martins Bank ornament: Midas with coins flowing from his beard

Water Street entrance: African child holding a money bag

Octopus sculpture on the façade of Martins Bank

Other bank projects

The project received considerable publicity, and Rowse was invited to develop a similar scheme in Barcelona for the Compania de Aplicacionas Electricas SA. Occupying a corner plot next to the church of Santa Anna, the project is similar in scale and approach to Martins Bank. The building is now occupied by the Banco de España and while Rowse's plans have been largely adhered to, it is not clear whether this was a speculative development with Rowse merely providing a concept layout. The tower flourish above the entrance that Rowse proposed was not built, and the façade treatment at ground level varies from the elevations.

Rowse sailed to Marseilles in 1930, perhaps en route to Barcelona in connection with the project, and this might also explain the presence of the *Exposición Internacional de Barcelona* catalogue in his sourcebook collection. The exhibition was held in 1929, and included Mies van der Rohe's famous pavilion, but it would appear Rowse was more interested in the Hungarian pavilion by Dénes György and Nikolaus Menyhért. This expressionist, Mayan-inspired structure, with its windowless tower and decoration at the cornice, appears to be a strong precedent for the Mersey Tunnel ventilation towers Rowse would go on to design in 1931.

Rowse also won commissions for smaller banks outside the commercial heart of Liverpool and designed a suburban branch in Childwall, described by Reilly as 'very pleasant in spite of its bulbous shape', as well as an intriguing 'mobile bank' for Martins made of steel, for use at fairs and exhibitions.[45] Although Reilly's conspicuous and pushy patronage did not waver, he was not altogether uncritical, and he seemed to be beckoning Rowse to abandon his Portland stone and penchant for classical solutions.

> The time was not ripe six years ago, even if it is now, for a purely modern expression in the very centre of a town. India Buildings, with its excellent straight forward plan round two courtyards, well finished and not left as lighting wells, with its corridors and halls, seems to hit off exactly that balance between purely mechanical efficiency and elegance, which the commerce of our day appears to call for. The exterior exhibits a clean veneer of stone to the steel frame, which, if it is slightly Italianized, is sufficiently plain to make all the surrounding buildings except the almost equally big one Rowse is himself erecting on the opposite side of the street, seem like over-flounced and beribboned old ladies.[46]

Rowse responded in a lecture to the Liverpool Architectural Society that 'there was no conscious striving after any particular style but rather the treatment was the outcome of the governing conditions which were imposed', namely the horizontal setbacks and a respect for the classical architecture of the town hall.[47]

Martins mobile bank, for use at fairs and exhibitions

Childwall branch of Lloyds Bank

It was a slow transition, and inertia of historical precedent was not easily overcome as Rowse again looked to Spain and the works of 16th-century architect Hernàn Ruiz II (c 1514–1569), and specifically his Palacio de los Villalones in Córdoba, for the Lloyds bank on Church Street, Liverpool. Rowse designed the Lloyd's bank interior at India Buildings, but 'on the rare occasions when Lloyds wished to be really different, as with Church Street, Liverpool branch, they first asked Reilly for his opinion'.[48] Reilly directed them, of course, to Rowse. The front façade borrows some of the Palacio's features, including the tripartite arch arrangement and a very similar decorative motif above and around the main entrance (by Tyson Smith and Edmund C Thompson).[49] Occupying a corner site of the city's main shopping street (so desirable by banks and public houses alike), the façade treatment wraps round onto the side street, further emphasising its 'hand-made, sand-faced bricks with cherry-red dressings and cream joints'.[50]

Lloyds Bank on Church Street, Liverpool City Centre 1930–31

Doorway of Lloyds Bank on Church Street (now removed)

The unusual façade becomes even more prominent as these materials contrast heavily with the sea of grey stone that forms the rest of the street. In using the same material for both front and side elevation, Rowse eliminated the unsightly switch that frequently occurs from the expensive front façade materials to the cheaper bricks on the side elevation. How did Rowse dodge the Corporation rule that all Church Street buildings should be faced in stone? It was a brave move, which, along with its turquoise-glazed roof tiles and elegant façade composition, sets the bank apart from its neighbours, commanding far more attention than such a small plot warrants.

Internally, there was a double-height banking hall, with an additional four storeys above for letting. The objective here was for the bank to stand out from the shopping displays, fashion and advertisements, and to offer a sense of history, permanence and respectability. Reilly regarded the building as possessing 'more dignity than the emporia of lingerie for which massive Greek columns have previously been the accepted architectural expression' – a comment on the proliferation of classically inspired department stores that had sprung up around the country following Selfridge's lead on London's Oxford Street some 20 years earlier. It was also sufficiently unorthodox to draw attention to itself, and was a pivotal project for Rowse – marking the transition from historical re-enactment and stone veneer towards extended brick surfaces enclosing geometric forms. While his use of decoration was always lyrical and playful, and rarely with any trace of a narrow subservience to a Greek classical order, his brick-faced work began to pursue abstract motifs and a new grammar of tessellating patterns, extrusions and stylised flat reliefs, drawing from the syncopated grammar of pseudo-Egyptian 'jazz-deco'. The ground floor of the Bank has been completely destroyed, with the loss of the elaborately carved Portland stone surround and Austrian oak doors that formed the entrance on Church Street. However, the original ornate ceiling to the double-height former banking hall is still intact.

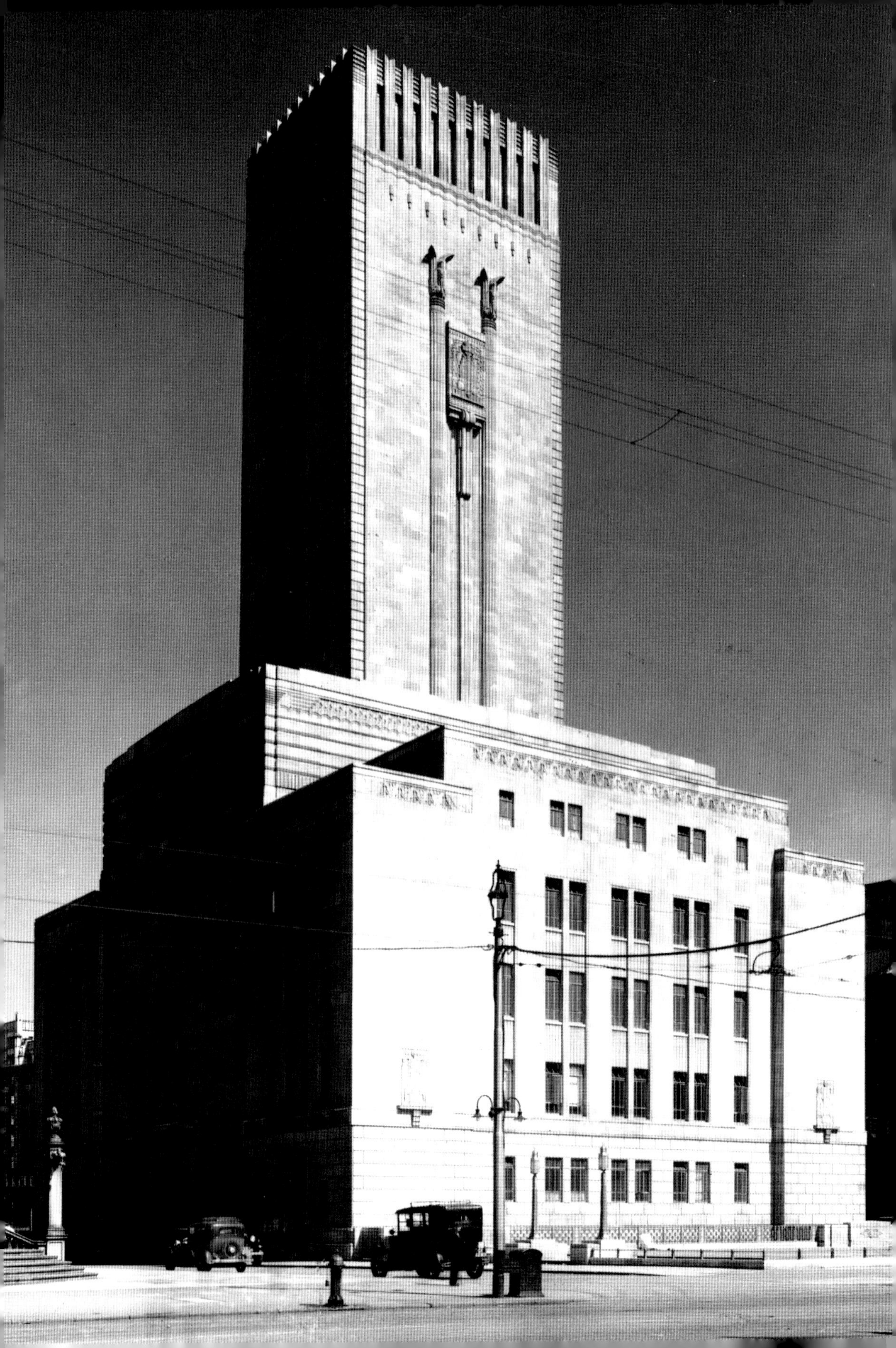

3 Tunnel structures

There was a desire for clear, rational planning in Rowse's work, and the practice strained to ensure that this underpinned all of the projects, often incorporating technical solutions into the early design decisions. According to Eric Hyde, 90 per cent of the design time was spent in researching and planning, with a series of adjustments being made until the final scheme emerged. Rowse liked to co-ordinate the structural and services design into this early part of the process, with the consultant engineers taking up temporary residence in Rowse's office to ensure everything was fully considered and integrated from the outset.[1] Once the scheme was resolved, it could then be very quickly transformed into a set of contract drawings. Competition entries were produced in the same manner and had a sense of completeness and competence as a result of this approach. It was this close allegiance with structural and building services engineers, and Rowse's ability to work creatively with them, that singled out the practice for complex traffic-management, tunnelling and ventilation, and civic-design projects.

The controversial history of the Mersey road tunnel

Ranking as one of the great municipal achievements of the inter-war years, the Mersey road tunnel was celebrated with pride by both Liverpool and Birkenhead when it was opened by King George V in 1934. Rowse's contribution to the later stages of this project included the design and styling of the tunnel interior and its approaches, as well as the construction of six massive ventilation stations, which became landmarks in the two cities. Before the architect was commissioned in early 1931, however, the project had not run smoothly. A few words may be helpful to explain the context within which this very public and politically highly charged commission came to an architect who was fast building a reputation for his technical and management skills.

Although later hailed as a triumph for municipal collaboration, the tunnel project had been dogged by controversy. Four Merseyside local authorities – Liverpool, Birkenhead, Bootle and Wallasey – had first combined to promote the project.[2] In 1922, the consortium commissioned a technical study by the former London County Council Chief Engineer Sir Maurice Fitzmaurice, working with Liverpool's City Engineer, John Brodie, and Basil Mott (later Sir Basil Mott, Baronet, FRS), one of Britain's top civil engineers, who stepped

Ventilation shaft at George's Dock

into the lead role when Fitzmaurice died. The engineers were tasked to study the feasibility and costs of a high-level bridge or a tunnel. Brodie was known to favour a bridge; Mott was probably Britain's foremost tunnelling expert with long experience of London's underground railway construction (including tube lines running under the Thames). Despite these differences, the experts reported in October 1923 unanimously in favour of a tunnel. A large-diameter circular-section tunnel with two entrances on each bank, four lanes of traffic running on the diameter, and two tram tracks on the lower level would cost £6,400,000. The estimate for a six-lane bridge (including two tram tracks) high enough to clear the tallest liners was £10,550,000 – and there were still many unanswered questions about how best to get motor vehicles and trams up to and down from a high-level bridge in the heavily developed waterfront districts.[3]

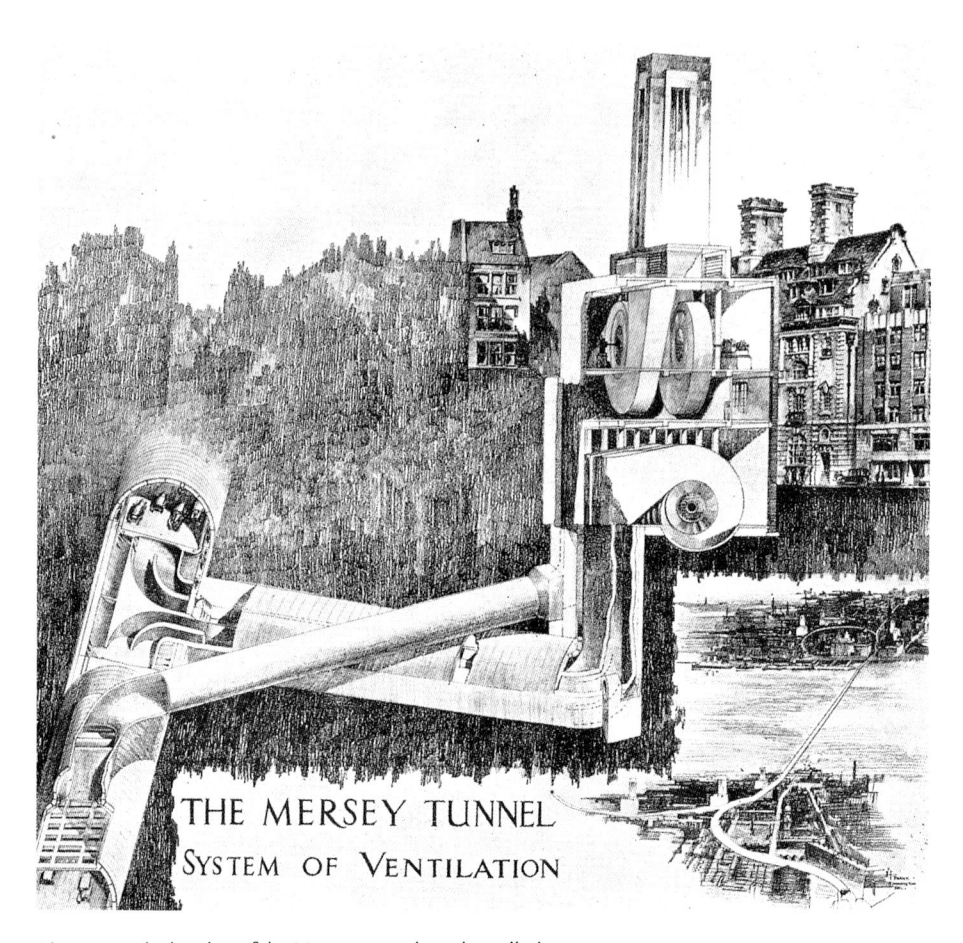

Diagrammatic drawing of the Mersey tunnels and ventilation towers

The consortium then formed a special tunnel subcommittee to secure the Parliamentary powers needed for the project. Before the Mersey Tunnel Act 1925 had been secured, however, Bootle's electorate had voted down their town's share of the project, and Wallasey had been excluded when that suburban borough had refused to pool its interests in the tram and cross-Mersey ferry enterprises, an important element in the consortium's planning. Following these removals, the project was trimmed to cut out the branch tunnel leading towards Wallasey, eliminating the trams, but leaving Birkenhead increasingly unhappy about a solution now based on a single entrance and exit complex. Birkenhead's discontents came close to derailing the project in its entirety, until eventually, a second branch on the Wirral side of the river was agreed, together with a change of location for the main entrance. Liverpool also witnessed controversy over the location and architectural treatment of the main downtown four-lane entry-and-exit complex, which had first been planned for Whitechapel, where it would have required considerable road widening and clearances in the heart of the business district. Not until 1928 were these fundamental arguments about the location of the tunnel entrances finally resolved.[4]

The entrance portals and toll-booth plazas at each end of the tunnel were not the only new elements in the urban landscape of Liverpool and Birkenhead. The engineers planned to ventilate the tunnel by pumping into it very large volumes of fresh air to dilute and drive out the carbon monoxide and other pollutants generated by motor traffic, using the tunnel itself as the exhaust duct. Technical evidence presented during the Parliamentary Select Committee hearings in 1925 made it clear that the system then proposed by Mott's team did not make use of the extract fans, ducts and flues employed in other contemporary tunnel projects, such as the so-called Holland Tubes already under construction between Manhattan and New Jersey.[5] Named for their engineer, Clifford Holland, who had died during their construction, the Holland Tubes took traffic under the Hudson river in two separate, one-way, two-lane tunnels. Each tube was ventilated through four tall stack towers, one on each bank and two more standing in the river at approximately the one-third and two-thirds points.[6] Basil Mott's Mersey tunnel was a single circular tube, roughly twice the diameter of each of Holland's tubes. This eventually made for a much less claustrophobic experience for Mersey tunnel users, but it incurred a much greater volume of pollutants to be shifted than in either of Holland's narrower tubes. It emerged much later (in unpublished confidential notes from 1932) that Mott's first proposals (probably datable to 1924 or perhaps very early 1925) included only two ventilation stations, one at Liverpool's Pierhead, the other beside Birkenhead's Woodside ferry landing stage.[7] By June 1925, the Lords Select Committee was told of five ventilation stations (three in Liverpool and two in Birkenhead). A sixth was added in the 1928 re-think, which gave Birkenhead its second entrance. At this stage, however, none of them included extract systems.

By 1929, doubts about the tunnel ventilation had evidently assailed Mott's team, and events in Pittsburgh were said to be at the root of these concerns. Pittsburgh's Liberty Tunnels had been completed in 1923, providing twin 6,000ft tubes under Mount Washington, and were linked directly over the Monongahela River into Pittsburgh's business district when the Liberty Bridge was completed in 1928. However, the tunnels were opened to traffic in January 1924, before the ventilation system was completed. On 10 May 1924, a rapid-transit strike brought extra cars into the city, jamming the tunnels. No one died, but many drivers, passengers and rescuers were overcome by fumes.[8]

Mott's team of engineers responded belatedly by undertaking ventilation and fire-fighting experiments in a completed 100-yard section of four-lane tunnel beneath Birkenhead's Hamilton Square. Although much of the archival record for the tunnel is missing (or perhaps was never deposited), it seems that the experiments carried out in 1930 and reported early in 1931 persuaded the engineers that extracts would be needed.[9] The ventilation stations were significantly increased in size and complexity to cope with the extract fans and their exhaust stacks. Costs were increased by this change, and by the decision to enlarge the toll-booth plazas outside the four Mersey tunnel entrances following reports from America of the traffic congestion created at each end of the Holland Tubes. Behind the scenes, a major cost crisis was mounting.

The bombshell news of massive cost increases broke publicly in December 1932, shocking the Merseyside public when it became known that the project was now short of £1.5 million.[10] The municipalities had to return to Parliament in 1933 (for the third time since 1925), seeking yet another new private act to cover the increased borrowing. Although the full extent of the shortfall was probably only partly appreciated when Rowse was appointed in early 1931, he took up his responsibilities at a difficult time. The excavation of the tunnel itself was still on track. However, the urban infrastructure of the tunnel openings was not designed and, if any plans for the ventilation stations existed, they were now subject to radical overhaul. Liverpool was fast becoming a high-rise city. The 1933 select committee of the Lords that heard the case for additional borrowing powers were told of the many high buildings recently built or under construction (some of the highest designed by Herbert Rowse himself) and the fears of 'noxious fumes' and threats of legal action by the owners of businesses near the ventilation stations. These, as Rowse's evidence to the Lords revealed, would now be built with double skins to minimise noise, and with intake and extract stacks built much higher than originally conceived.[11] Public opinion and the tunnel committee demanded designs worthy of such an ambitious civic undertaking.

By 1933, Parliament could hardly refuse the additional borrowing powers, because to do so would frustrate a project now seen as a key part of the Government's renewal programme for the North West. This said, the Select Committees of 1933 were not simply rubber stamps. The engineers and their employers, the Mersey Tunnel Joint Committee, were pressed to explain how the project's costs had escalated so embarrassingly above the earlier estimates. The revised costings show those responsible wriggling wildly as they massaged the figures to conceal (or at any rate disguise) the full extent of the design changes. Sir Basil Mott was too ill to attend the Select Committee hearings, and the technical presentations were handled by Bertram Hewett (the site engineer in charge), who drew attention to the pioneering nature of the project and the many uncertainties that had driven the engineers originally to roll up all of the ventilation costs into a massive 23 per cent contingency sum. The Bill was approved, and the building programme went into overdrive to complete the above-ground structures before the royal opening, now planned for the summer of 1934. Rowse embarked on what was probably the most high-pressure burst of professional activity yet seen in his career.

Above-ground structures: ventilation towers and tunnel openings

In April 1931, the Mersey Tunnel Joint Committee had announced that it would not concern itself with the tunnel entrances on each side of the river: this would be a matter for the two corporations of Liverpool and Birkenhead, both of whom then approved the appointment of Rowse, although it was made clear that the architect was working under the instructions of Basil Mott.[12] As soon as drawings indicating the proposed architectural treatment became available, Merseyside's newspapers scrambled to publish them. Rowse's scheme for the Rendel Street [dock] entrance in Birkenhead appeared in May 1931 in a striking air-view.[13] More perspectives of Birkenhead's city-centre entrance appeared in July 1932, and in September of the same year, the first of Rowse's perspectives of the Pierhead ventilation station and control centre were published locally and in the national architectural press.[14]

The Pierhead ventilation structure sat on land owned by the Docks and Harbour Board, situated prominently between the Harbour Board's building and the Dock Road. The Harbour Board had insisted on high-quality architecture to sit comfortably next door to its own building and close to the two others that formed Liverpool's 'Three Graces'. Many today believe that Rowse's building is the most sophisticated of the Pierhead group. It is certainly different, largely windowless but with elegant Art Deco low-relief decoration not only on its ashlar external surfaces but also on many of the interior ones, despite this being, in reality, an industrial building. However, the site constraints presented Rowse with a complex design problem. With its intake and extract tower, tunnel control room and offices of the future Joint Tunnel Company forming a base, the structure had been squeezed onto a surprisingly restricted site.

Sketches of the ventilation towers

View of George's Dock ventilation tower from the Royal Liver Building

It needed to sit beside (rather than directly above) the tunnel, which ran beneath the road separating the Harbour Board and Cunard Building, while avoiding an old dock that had been filled in the 19th century and that the structural engineers did not now wish to see excessively loaded. Hence the two gardens flanking Rowse's building and the promise that they would be maintained as landscaped open space.

As Parliament had already heard, the towers had been increased in height (under pressure from neighbouring building owners) and the original single-skin envelope had been redesigned as a double wall to reduce noise from the fans.[15] The prestigious Dock Road structure and the ventilation station on North John Street in the central business district would both be faced with stone, adding further weight. Most of the outer walls would be blind, again to reduce noise, but adding yet more weight. At a late stage in the approval process, a small adjustment was needed to the placement of the building's foundations. At the same time, the tall windows lighting the offices on the Dock Road façade were replaced by a reduced number of smaller windows on the short plinth façades (giving some privacy in the offices from the trains on the elevated railway that ran along the Dock Road serving Liverpool's waterfront).

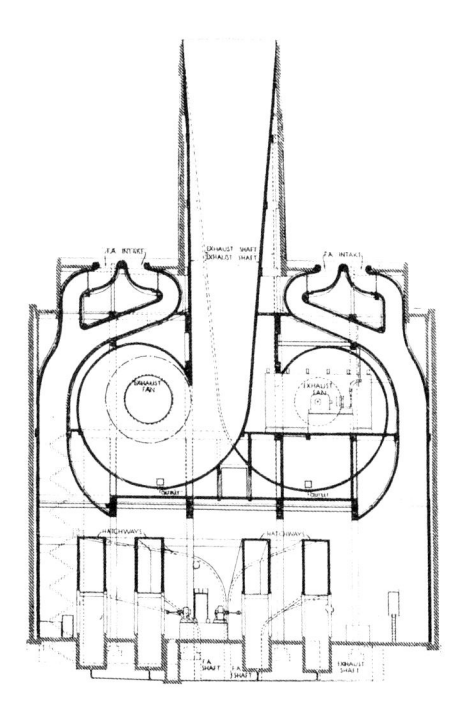

Section of ventilation shaft, George's Dock

Decorative motifs on North John Street ventilation tower

The decoration of the Pierhead tower was lavish. The George's Dock Way frontage contains a large carved relief, designed by Rowse and executed by Thompson and Capstick, entitled 'Speed'. It consists of an extremely stylised tall streamlined figure that is symmetrical along its vertical axis. Apart from the head, which is wearing a motor-racing helmet and raised goggles, all human characteristics are eliminated in order to emphasise the vertical lines – presenting an image of motorised speed. The tower is also adorned with a number of other sculptural reliefs and free-standing sculptures. 'Night' and 'Day', both by Thompson in black basalt, are intended to convey the never-closing nature of the tunnel. In addition, there are four large reliefs, one on each of the building's façades – 'Civil Engineering', 'Construction', 'Architecture' and 'Decoration' – together with a repeated relief on all four façades entitled 'Ventilation' that consists of a symmetrical design based on a ventilator shaft blowing out vitiated air, represented by a stylised Art Deco-inspired zigzag pattern.

Dramatic forms and abstract decoration on George's Dock tower

TUNNEL STRUCTURES

'Speed' sculpture on George's Dock ventilation shaft

'Day' sculpture on George's Dock ventilation shaft

Lamp and decoration on George's Dock ventilation tower

'Egyptian' motifs and decoration on the George's Dock ventilation tower

The complex planning and ornamentation caused further delay, and the Pierhead building was the only one of the six not to be completed before the formal opening of the tunnel by the king on 18 July 1934. Temporary fan systems were installed to allow the tunnel itself to open. Rowse had explained all of these difficulties to the 1933 Parliamentary Committees and repeated the key points in a rare public lecture to the Liverpool Architectural Society in April 1934.[16] The meeting was chaired by Professor Lionel Budden, who had recently succeeded Reilly as head of the University School of Architecture. 'No architect at any time had so transformed the silhouette on both sides of the river,' declared Budden amid a chorus of praise from his fellow architects. Budden then spoilt it by complaining about architects so often being asked to put clothes on engineers' designs, when Rowse had stated here (as well as to the Parliamentary Committee in 1933) that all aspects of the ventilation stations had been under his personal control from the start of his commission in 1931. Rowse himself may have exaggerated slightly here, because a photograph published in the 1930 pamphlet reporting an official visit to the tunnel by the Joint Tunnel Committee and their guests showed the steel frame of the North John Street station already rising over the rooftops. This would seem to suggest that something had been designed before Rowse was commissioned. But no-one seems to have noticed and Rowse deserves credit for an unusually comprehensive personal involvement in the design of all six ventilation stations, the four tunnel entrances and the internal finishes and detailing of the tunnel itself, which – unlike the portals and ventilation structures – had until now been seen only by civic leaders and their official guests.

Engaging public support and the opening of the tunnel

Well before the 1932 cost crisis and the enforced return to Parliament, the tunnel promoters had begun a campaign to engage the public with the delayed project. In March 1931, Bertram Hewett lectured on the tunnel and its ventilation to the Liverpool Traffic Club.[17] A scaled sectional model of the whole tunnel went on public view in Lewis's department store in April. The model had been made by Partridges Ltd of London at a cost of £1,000. It was 4.5m (15ft) long and mounted on a bridge, with catwalks for viewers at high and low level. The model tunnel itself had a bore of two inches (indicating that the vertical and horizontal dimensions were somewhat enlarged). It was lit by tiny electric lights and miniature cars moved through it.[18] The store later displayed a large architectural model of Liverpool's Haymarket entrance.[19]

The real campaign high points, however, followed the decision to open the tunnel to the public in December 1933. The tunnel itself had been practically completed by then – well before the delayed ventilation structures – and the Committee (no doubt with Pittsburgh's lessons in mind) had resisted demands to let traffic begin using it without working ventilation. The first pedestrian walk-through was a massive success: 34,000 people each paid 6d to crowd through the tunnel, the turnstiles manned by unemployed ex-servicemen and the proceeds going to the Goodfellow Fund for Liverpool hospitals.[20] Another four-day opening over the Easter weekend of 1934 again drew enormous crowds: 181,000 visitors were recorded on the first three days, with an 'invasion from Manchester' expected on Easter Monday.[21] A letter from the Revd J J R Armitage of Christ Church, Great Homer Street, protested against 'this organised dissipation on Sunday'.[22] His was a lone voice.

By now, the local press was beginning to anticipate the festival planned for the royal opening. The Lord Mayor held a design competition for street decorations, open to Liverpool students of art and architecture and assessed by Rowse, Professors Abercrombie and Budden and Mr H P Huggill, principal of the School of Art. The competition was won by Mr H J Gordon, a student at the University School of Architecture, with a design for tall standards bearing liver-bird motifs and long streamers. In Castle Street, masts designed by another Liverpool architecture student, Lawrence Wright, and previously used for the king's 1927 visit, were brought out again with new banners. The Seven Lamps of the Town Hall became the theme for a medieval pageant featuring the commercial life of Liverpool, with processional floats carrying the daughters of some of Liverpool's leading citizens and of the Rear Admiral commanding the Navy training ship.[23] It all added up to an interesting mixture (or was it a clash?) of styles: medieval pageantry, street pylons and banners of the type favoured by Europe's dictators, Art Deco in stone or brick for the ventilation stations, and robust stone portals with sculptured motifs leading into a tunnel interior with a machine-age sleek black-glass dado and a smooth 'broken white' vault forming an elegant semicircular skin above a textured steel roadway.

On 18 July 1934, King George V opened the East Lancashire Road, the Mersey road tunnel and the new central public library in Birkenhead, replacing the Carnegie central library, which had been demolished to make room for the city-centre tunnel-entrance plaza. After the royal motorcade had driven through the tunnel, more than 80,000 pedestrians followed, enjoying a final walk-through. This was probably the best way to appreciate Rowse's detailed design, offering close-up views of Thompson and Capstick's low-relief carvings located above the entrance portals, as well as the commemorative plaques on the granite columns. Inside the tunnel, everything was slickly modern. The raised precast non-slip footways housing the air input vents were made by the Liverpool Artificial Stone company, who also manufactured the spun concrete lamp standards at the Birkenhead toll plaza. The glass dado (by Mellowes and Co Ltd of Sheffield) was mounted on rails set far enough out from the steel and injected-concrete tunnel lining to provide for movement as well as space for the 600 miles of 'Mersylite' insulated cabling to the 2,500 lights, 94 fire-alarm boxes and the neon traffic-control signage (which controlled the junctions to the smaller 8m/26ft-wide tunnels).

Decorations installed for the tunnel opening celebrations

Drawing of tunnel entrance, lighting and pylons at Liverpool

Aerial view of Birkenhead tunnel entrance

A stone mason carving the Mersey Tunnel entrance stone

These and many other subcontracts had all been delegated to Rowse as the tunnel architect by Sir Basil Mott and, in turn, subcontracted by him to specialist firms – who made much of them in subsequent advertising. Rowse also designed the fan casings concealed in the ventilation towers, which were made in polished precast concrete by the Trussed Concrete Steel Company. The *Architectural Review* coverage of the scheme dwelt lovingly on these almost biological shapes, while the *Illustrated London News* provided some of the most dramatic photographs of the ventilation tower exteriors – calling them 'Castles of the Air' – and was much taken with the 18.2m (60ft) -high black-granite shaft (with entasis) that marked each tunnel entrance with its lotus-shaped bowl: 'A Pillar of Light'.[24] The shafts contained a ladder for lighting maintenance. The *Radio Times* (13 July 1934) showcased the tunnel interiors, but probably the most detailed account of the servicing and ventilation systems was to be found in *The Times Trade and Engineering Supplement* (28 April 1934).[25] Coverage by these widely read nonspecialist publications proved a source of future commissions for the architect: indeed shortly afterwards, Rowse would be commissioned to design a new headquarters buildings and laboratory for the St Helens glass manufacturer, Pilkington's, as well as new premises, training school and laboratories for the Pharmaceutical Society in London. For the tunnel project and its civic promoters, this kind of coverage reached a far wider readership than any amount of praise from the professional architectural or engineering press.

The tunnel entrance portals were clad in Portland Stone with delicate cornices and geometric carved decoration adorning the sweeping flanks that spill out from the tunnel portal. In addition to the Pillars of Light, other smaller structures include triumphal arches placed at the limits of the approach roads, providing shelter to the toll-booth staff as well as first aid facilities. The toll booths were emerald and gold kiosks of cast-iron with a glazed upper-section and perimeter lighting cove. These neatly formed miniature buildings (probably inspired by the transportable Martins bank buildings designed by Rowse for the bank's public face at events) were Rowse's smallest commissions.

Triumphal arches or pylons at the tunnel entrances

TUNNEL STRUCTURES

Mersey Tunnel toll booth

Birkenhead Woodside ventilation shaft looking towards Liverpool

At the other end of the scale was the colossal Birkenhead Woodside ventilation tower, almost perched over the water near the Mersey ferry landing stages. Unlike the other five ventilation buildings, which share the same 'turret' motif while occupying unique bases, the Woodside variation had to take a different approach due to its close proximity to the river. This slender structure, located just 5.7m (19ft) from the river wall and on a very restricted site, forced a dramatic tower solution, offering a formidable outline at 65m (213ft) tall, and highly visible when viewed from across the river. The symmetry found in all the designs was due to the internal arrangement of the fan machinery, installed in duplicate should any of the components break down. Located alongside the fans are two shafts, providing intake and exhaust air, which had to be kept separate, the exhaust no contaminating the inlet and discharging at an appropriate distance from surrounding buildings. The machinery is supported on a steel frame, which also provides the main structure for the façades. Woodside again caused considerable difficulty as so much of the interior volume had to be kept clear of 'structure' to enable the fans and ducts to be installed, coupled with the extreme loads placed on a building of this height with a depth of just 12m (39ft).

Birkenhead Woodside ventilation shaft in the near distance and Sydney Street ventilation shaft at right, viewed from Liverpool

TUNNEL STRUCTURES

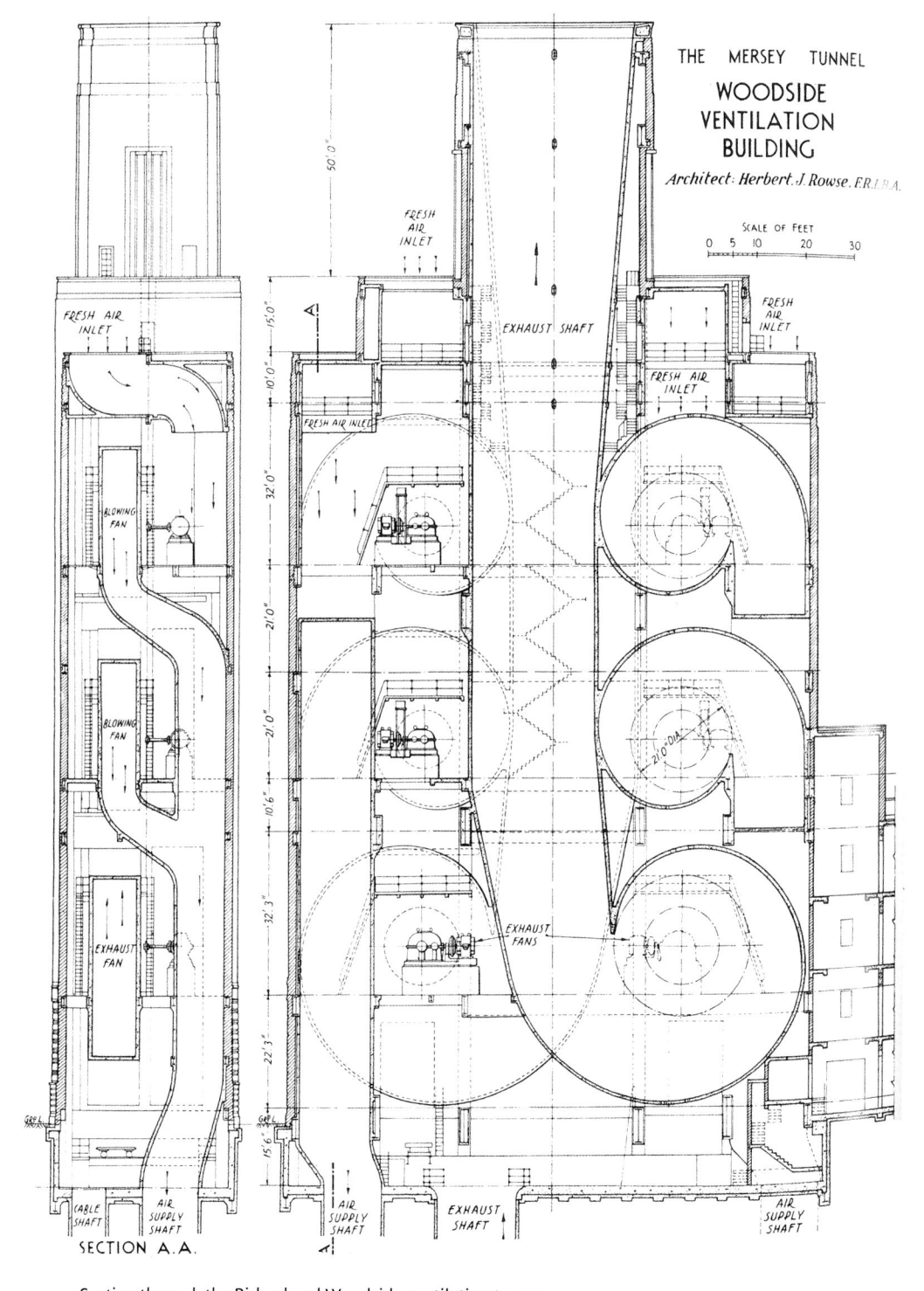

Section through the Birkenhead Woodside ventilation tower

TUNNEL STRUCTURES

The structure had to carry the considerable strain of the machinery as well as resist wind loads and the weight of the masonry walls. A solution was found by casting concrete stanchions in each corner of the structure taken down 12m (39ft) to bedrock. The brickwork, laid with flush mortar joints, gives a bold monolithic impression, with vast surfaces left plain. At the corners and cornices, the bricks are laid in bands of proud, recessed and edge-on courses to form discrete but very effective patterns in a monochromatic palette.

The ventilation structures are all so carefully composed that it is easy to forget they are the casements for functioning machines. Frederic Towndrow goes even further, imbuing them as living things, 'like huge animals, breathing out at the top and breathing-in just below the top ... there is nothing like them in the world', indeed they sit, silently, and seemingly without any human interaction ensuring a subterranean existence below.[26]

Brick details at the Birkenhead Woodside ventilation tower

Birkenhead Woodside ventilation tower

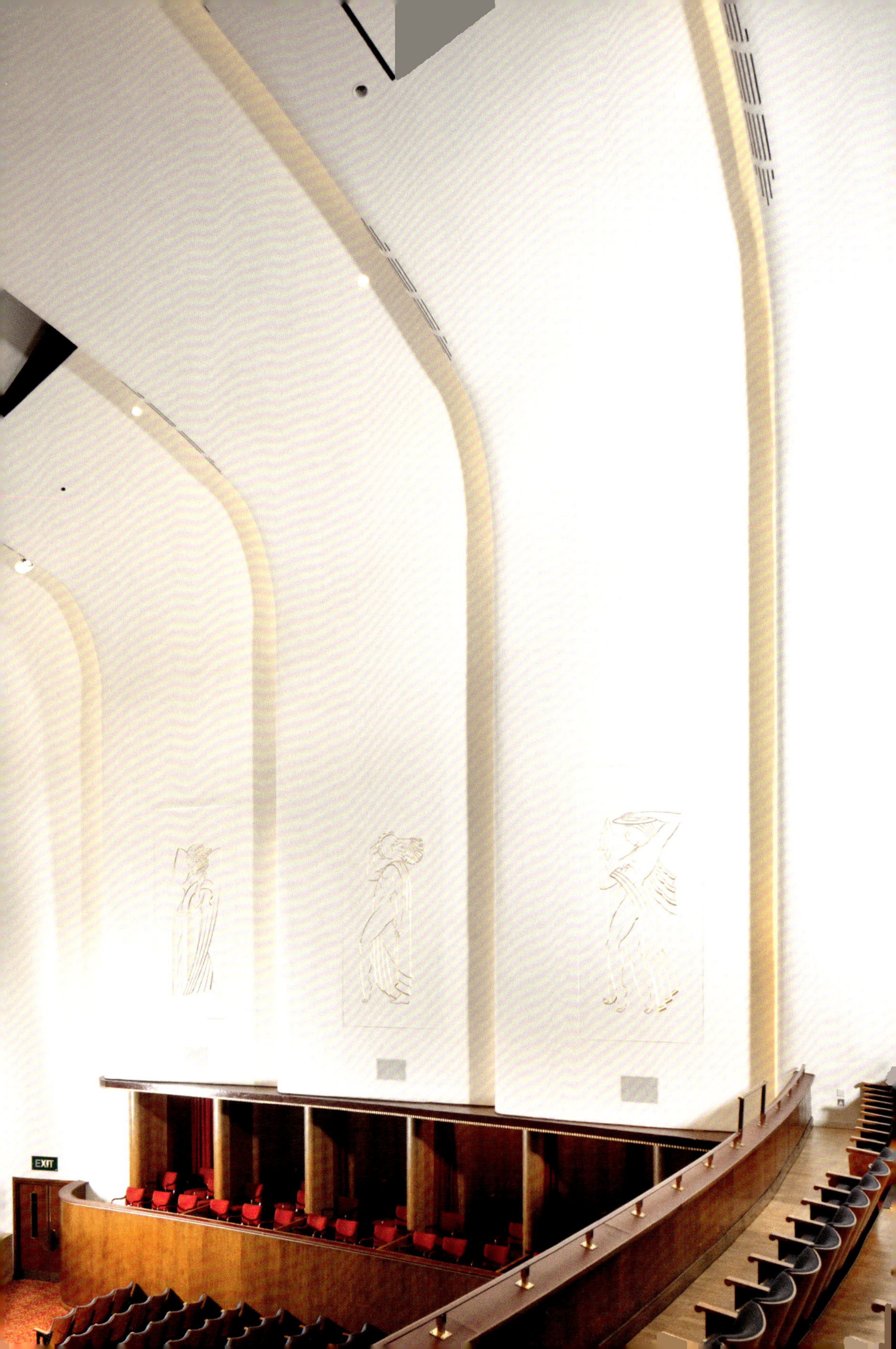
EXIT

4 Brick

The ventilation towers were the first of Rowse's major buildings to be fully presented as fair-faced brickwork since the Manbré and Garton factory of 1919. His interest in brick may have been rekindled by the Dutch projects now being published, or even by the Hungarian pavilion from the 1929 Barcelona International Exhibition, which had impressed him. By the mid-1930s, Rowse was poised to undertake a number of commissions for technically advanced buildings quite different from the commercial structures that had brought him success, and all exploiting the potential decorative qualities of brickwork.

While it may seem that Rowse made a sudden switch from corporate classicism of Portland stone to a more modernist approach of brick geometric forms, this would be oversimplifying the case. Rowse continued to work in brick throughout the 1920s and early 1930s, as his factories, banks, flats and some of his most prominent tunnel ventilation towers reveal – and there was no dramatic transfiguration towards a modernist creed. Instead, Rowse pursued an incremental, tentative yet deliberate adjustment towards working in these large cubic masses and interlocking rectilinear forms. He displayed extreme confidence in using brick, preferring to express its weight and compressive load-bearing character than to flaunt the nimble leaps of the steel frame hidden behind. Brickwork also contained enough variety and texture to be used across large areas, which would have appeared overly stark and hard in ashlar. Considerable homage was paid in the later brick-faced work to Swedish and Dutch pioneers, and Rowse had clearly been impressed by the Hungarian pavilion from the 1929 Barcelona International Exhibition. The Continental Modernists, however, reflected their exterior simplicity into the interior spaces, where Rowse continued to crave something more opulent. His was an approach that grated against the growing trend of functionalism and MARS group ambitions. When reviewing the Glasgow Empire Exhibition, Reilly thought Rowse's approach 'is not as good as it might have been ... the building seems, both by its exterior forms and by its interior vaulting, to imitate a heavy masonry structure rather than to express a light one of steel'.[1] Rowse did not deem it necessary to 'express' such things; it was the overall effect, the mass and material qualities that would stimulate an emotional response and connection to the work, rather than a deference to 'honest' structural exposure.

Liverpool Philharmonic Hall

The Philharmonic Hall

Liverpool gasped its way through the hot summer of 1933 until one sultry night in July saw the tragic end of the old Philharmonic Hall. It was a building admired by both locals and visitors alike and famous the world over, but once fire had taken a hand, it survived only a matter of hours.[2]

Designed by the architect of Liverpool Lime Street station John Cunningham (1799–1873) in 1844, the design was considered acoustically flawless, but according to the *Liverpolitan*, nothing survived the blaze other than some scores left blowing in the wind and the contents of the safe.[3] The Liverpool Philharmonic Society had formed in 1840, and the lament for the hall ran deep, for this was more than just a gathering space, and 'all that it meant in the social and cultural amenities of the city, seemed to have passed away'.[4]

With the charred remains yet to cool, the Philharmonic Society immediately began contemplating its future and a new venue. It possessed a prime site on Hope Street, directly facing the Blind School extension (1931) by Spencely and Minoprio and the Edwardian Baroque frenzy that is the Philharmonic Dining Rooms (1898), and the City Corporation was equally eager for the project to be a major success. Discussions considered a broader remit, including 'a public meeting-place devoted primarily to music and, at the same time, available for other purposes.'[5] A collaboration with the City Corporation would have brought financial security for the Philharmonic but at the cost of independence, plus a multipurpose hall would likely compromise the acoustic properties of the venue. After six years of extended discussions and searches for a new site, the talks ended in frustration, with the Society nomadically squatting at other venues and rehearsal spaces in the meantime.[6] The conductor Sir Henry Wood gave an extended tirade on the situation and was adamant that

> Music should not be mixed up with anything else. There are scores of places where people can dance and have their pizazz. Let Liverpool have its social centre, let the Council put it up for them but for goodness' sake don't make the fundamental and unforgivable mistake of thinking that the cause of music would be served by simply allocating a bit of it to the Philharmonic.[7]

Finally, the Philharmonic Society decided it would develop the old site alone, using its £80,000 insurance payment, for as Sir Henry noted, 'music is not entertainment. It is education in its highest sense'.[8] Opting for an entirely seated 2,200-capacity venue rather than a general-purpose hall limited the rental potential, but it enabled a custom design with calibrated acoustic properties and high-quality fixed seating.

Like many halls from the 19th century, the first venue was closely modelled on Leipzig's Gewandhaus, but the new design broke from this precedent and utilised the latest scientific acoustic projections and measurements, releasing the new

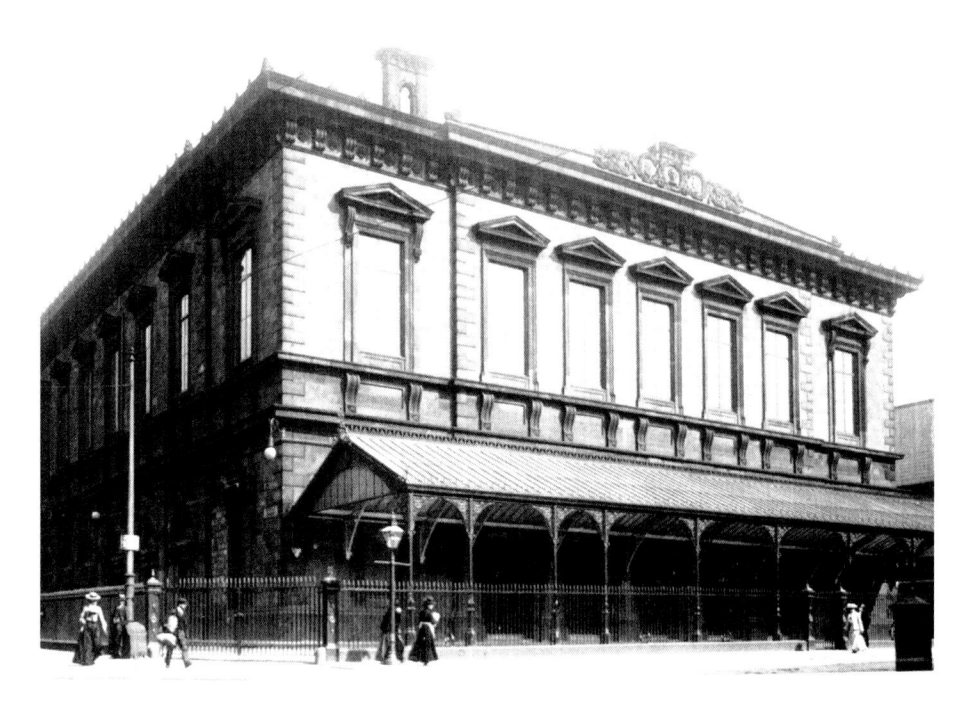

The old Philharmonic Hall, Liverpool

The old Philharmonic Hall on fire

project 'from any necessity for a blind conformity to the traditional form'.[9] This climatic computational engineering of the interior was, 'not only the basis of new standards of convenience and comfort, but also of original aesthetic values, having a peculiar authenticity in our own period'.[10] The delays in rebuilding resulted in the Society's decision to appoint an architect directly rather than hold a competition, and they plumped straight for Rowse, appointing him on 23 December 1935. It was exactly the type of project that Rowse enjoyed and excelled at, combining advanced building services, complex circulation paths, large occupancy figures and a strong civic presence with flamboyant, rich interiors. However, unlike the banks and offices with their extensive building funds, the budget needed some judicious deployment, and the existing basement walls were retained where possible as non-structural partitions.[11] Rowse produced some sketches for the Philharmonic committee's approval, which were exhibited at the Bluecoat Chambers, with Rowse alongside to answer questions.[12] The designs were approved, but Rowse noted he had only budgeted for 'the lowest possible standard of building permissible under the City byelaws ... the exterior of the building was shown in the cheapest quality bricks, and no decorative features for the interior had been included'.[13] The committee agreed that the budget could be stretched to improve the material choices, decorative features and the grand foyer door, plus, in a concession to attracting new and larger audiences, they decided to 'equip the Hall with appropriate sound-film projection apparatus', believing it would also 'serve the cause of education in the city'.[14] Rowse relished this opportunity and opted for the latest Walturdaw cinema screen, whose seven tons would rise from beneath the stage along with an organ console. This was typical of Rowse's penchant for integrated building services, and he also introduced air conditioning, ducted from roof level and piped into the hall, wiring for telephones, and an automated vacuum-cleaning plant.[15]

The windowless auditorium space was expressed on the exterior as large expanses of slender rusty-brown brickwork, arranged in strong interlocking geometric forms. The humble brick was writ large and laid in a straightforward manner with none of the flourishes used on the sugar refinery and the tunnel ventilation shafts. It forms a strong confident bluff to the giddy abandon of the Dining Rooms opposite, while reflecting the restraint and ornamental approach of the Blind School (with high-relief sculptures by John Skeaping). Dutch architect Willem Marinus Dudok is frequently cited as an important influence, and the Hilversum Town Hall (1928–31) clearly sets the tone for the Philharmonic.[16] This work would surely have been familiar to Rowse, as Dudok was awarded the RIBA Gold Medal in 1935, and Rowse's assistant, Alwyn Edward Rice, had produced a very Dudokian student thesis project for a concert hall just a couple of years earlier.[17] The Philharmonic Hall contributed to something of a modernist brick resurgence in the city during the 1930s, alongside St Andrew's Gardens by John Hughes, Wavertree Gardens housing,

Proposed Concert Hall, student project by A E Rice

and Speke Airport by Edward Bloomfield. These projects all adopted brick with occasional concrete dressings to create refined, crisp and charged works filled with an assured optimism and fresh stance. The Philharmonic Hall is, however, a much more sculpted, formal composition than these projects, and its 'island site' and elevated position offer uninterrupted views of the façades and overall massing. The symmetrical front façade breaks up the stark dovetailing cuboids and is further softened by the expanse of windows facing into the buffet bar at first-floor level and by the hemispherical staircase projections with narrow vertical fenestration. At street level, the weight of the imposing masonry mass above is lessened by the glazed elements and delicate sweep of the cantilevered concrete marquise above the entrance. The design was not without its detractors, however, and several letters were sent to the Building Committee expressing various concerns, not least about the lack of windows on the side elevations, as a member of Liverpool Engineering Society grumbled:

I consider the custom of sealing up buildings is due to the rapid growth of the Cinema ... I anticipate, however, that there will, in buildings other than cinemas, be a return to sanity, in the matter of light and fresh air, and that in the not far distant future we will no longer crawl in like moles to a tunnel to seek our amusements.[18]

Perhaps daylight would have made the hall more attractive to potential external users, and the Church Mission Society did complain about insufficient light to read the hymn sheets, but Rowse and the Building Committee stuck to their own mission, which was to provide the best acoustic environment for orchestral and choral works, something that fenestration would have impaired.

The interior was composed of only the finest materials, 'consistent with the best contemporary continental practice'. A shallow staircase from the entrance

Exterior view of the Philharmonic Hall

crush-hall leads to the continuous concrete shell of the auditorium, which is composed of a series of large nesting hoops that merge wall and ceiling into one flowing element (Rowse likened it to a megaphone). The gaps between the hoops contain the ventilation ducts and concealed lighting to the chamber, as well as ingeniously obscuring the organ pipes at stage level. Rowse imagined the effect of the hall when illuminated to be 'one of a succession of glowing facets of graded light on suave sculptural forms'.[19] The stage can hold a full orchestra with space for guest and solo performers, and the Walturdaw rising cinema screen[20] gives a sense of drama and excitement as it emerges from the stage with the organ providing accompaniment prior to the start of a film. It is a highly refined interior without compromise, the slightly raking floors offering every seat a clear view of the stage, while the boxes (panelled in ash and Indian laurel) are 'planned to lie within the area of maximum acoustical efficiency'.[21]

The Philharmonic Hall auditorium

Auditorium, stage and murals on the flank walls

BRICK

The Philharmonic Hall box seats

The somewhat abrupt exterior is completely countered by the opulence of the interior, where every edge is chamfered, and curved 'fluid' surfaces create a tactile and immersive realm focused completely on the stage, so that 'the mind may rest undistracted from the musical performance'.[22] The permission to increase the budget enabled Rowse to commission various pieces of decoration for the Hall, but unlike the sculptures and ornament of the banks, tunnels and offices, the Philharmonic was adorned with murals and ornamental glazing.

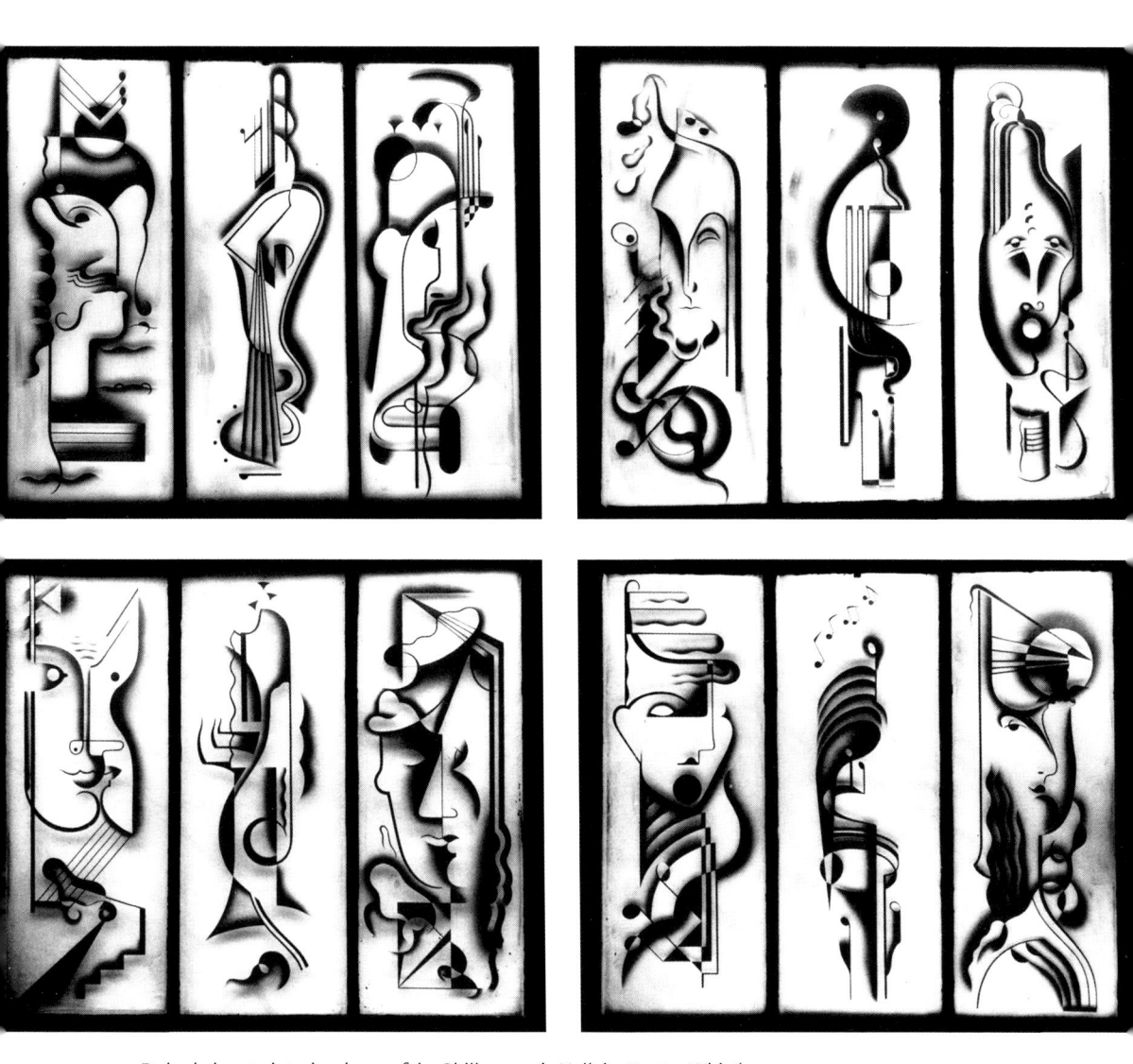

Etched glass to interior doors of the Philharmonic Hall, by Hector Whistler

The windows in the Grand Foyer and the panels in the entrance doorways are decorated with etched glass by Reginald Hector Whistler,[23] and the tale of Apollo being instructed by Pan is depicted on panels designed by Edmund Thompson (who also carved the figures at St George's Dock Ventilation Tower). Thompson also painted the six incised panels of dancing female figures that line the auditorium walls. The entrance hall contains a repoussé copper memorial to the musicians of the *Titanic* by Josef A Hodel.[24]

Apollo being instructed by Pan mural, by Edmund Thompson

Pilkington's head office, canteen and showrooms

In the summer of 1931, Pilkington, the large glass-manufacturing firm based in St Helens, had reorganised its old partnership structure, moving from a private family firm with informal processes towards an Executive Committee with management structures and systems fit for a large international modern company. As well as investment into research and product development, this saw the creation of a 'Planning and Propaganda' group led by Geoffrey Pilkington (Chairman of the Board) and strongly under the influence and direction of 'design promoter' John Gloag (of Pritchard, Wood and Partners). With Geoffrey Pilkington, he developed an extraordinary three-pronged 'propaganda' (what we would now call marketing) campaign, with showrooms, a converted LNER train-coach travelling exhibition and a large glossy publication expounding all things glass and freely distributed to architects and glass merchants.[25] It formed part of an agenda to stimulate increased glazing in construction and was promulgated as 'The Glass Age'; indeed, this was the slogan used by Pilkington in their advertising campaigns. It was a timely approach that saw Pilkington well placed to weather the economic instability of the early 1930s.[26]

The management changes resulted in greater organisation and less ad hoc processes, coupled with a greater degree of centralisation of research and development, as well as a move from merely supplying technical advice to becoming the taste-makers and innovators in design solutions. They created an architectural department in 1933, led by Kenneth Cheeseman and chief designer Sigmund Pollitzer (1913–82).[27] Cheeseman and Pollizter were responsible for designing the 'glass train' exhibition and the showroom fit-outs, as well as advising architects and designers wishing to use the new product ranges. Hector Whistler was also on the staff (and, as previously mentioned, designed the Philharmonic Hall entrance doors).[28]

The new product ranges were added mainly through acquiring smaller companies and manufacturing rights to American-developed products. Licences from the Vitrolite Construction Company were bought in 1932 (producing a rolled opal glass with the trade name Vitrolite) and Insulight™, a glass block. These products were heavily promoted not only through the showrooms and exhibitions but also through the company's own developments, such as their hotel in Kirk Sandall, externally clad in 8mm-thick Vitrolite in a variety of bold and contrasting colours.[29] Kirk Sandall was a company town for Pilkington's Doncaster works, initially planned by Patrick Abercrombie, while the individual housing and amenities were designed by T H Johnson and Son.[30] (Johnson's friend William Crabtree, who as a recent graduate was later recommended by Reilly to work on Peter Jones in London, was employed here prior to attending Liverpool University.) Johnson was also commissioned to design the Doncaster offices using brick and the new glass products.

He developed some innovative cantilevered canopies with glass-block infill to allow daylight penetration, but the remainder of the project was dryly utilitarian.

In a similar vein, new premises were desired for St Helens to reflect the new management structure and to move away from the company's forsaken headquarters, which had been built in 1888 and extended in 1908. Arnold Thornley (Rowse's collaborator on India Buildings) was initially appointed to design the extension, but, disillusioned with his excessive ceiling heights and Stormontesque approach, Pilkington sought a more progressive image and to use their own products to greater effect.[31] The chief advocate for replacing Thornley was the recently appointed Cheeseman, who was strongly steering the directors towards modernist works such as the Daily Express building and Peter Jones department store, with their extensive and innovative use of glass and black Vitrolite. The radical ensemble known as the Glass Age Committee[32] were also publishing their adventurous and confident projects in the architectural press, sparking a debate about how glass might be used for more than just conventional fenestration. Vitrolite was eagerly adopted for use in bars, cafés and cinema applications, where its bold colour palette, flexible installation and signage potential was relished, but the major endorsement was the cladding of the Mersey Tunnel interiors (with photographs featuring in both the Vitrolite specification book and glass book).[33]

This vast order would have certainly made Pilkington aware of Rowse, and as the company desired to work with locally based architects, he was deemed an ideal choice to, again, take over from Thornley. In 1934, Rowse was invited to submit plans for a combined office and canteen block.[34] It was to be a two-storey building connected to the existing head office, with a budget of almost £50,000. The canteen was to be completed within 12 months and cost £32,000. Rowse was under strict instruction to be as economical as possible and not to provide excess accommodation, but, to give some context and an indication of priorities, the advertising budget reached £20,000 per year between 1936 and 1938,[35] and 3,000 copies of the specially commissioned *Glass in Architecture and Decoration* were printed and distributed to architects and glass merchants.[36] The canteen, seating 520, had a reinforced-concrete frame, delivering a clear span of just over 18m, with the walls clad in mottled-green glass to dado height and the same material repeated on the table tops.

The canteen offered high-quality facilities for the office staff, but the real extravagance was saved for the main building, where the entrance hall had specially made fluted-glass pilasters, complete with integrated lighting. The pilasters were abutted to a ribbed-glass wall panel that 'spreads the effect of the light along the wall surface'.[37] It was a neat solution and a move towards factory-based fit-outs and 'dry' finishing of interiors without the need for plasterwork and painted decoration. Glass blocks were used more widely and combined with a concrete structure to form a barrel-vault over the garage.

The dramatic photographs by Stewart Bale give the effect of an insect's ommatidia eye, particularly when viewed from the interior. The blocks offered the means to illuminate underground spaces, while generating a striking, resilient hard-landscaping above, and had just received accreditation from the Building Research Establishment in 1932 for their fire-resistant properties, opening up a new way of building semi-transparent walls, ceilings and canopies.[38]

Main entrance to Pilkington headquarters, St Helens

Curved façade of new Pilkington office building

Pilkington staff canteen

Garage showing glazed-block roof

If the everyday spaces had an augmented treatment, the showrooms were an over-excited frenzy. There were no constraints placed on the quantity of glazed products and associated specialist treatments to be applied. The Sheet Works Showroom went to the limits, and took an intrepid, even overstated approach that would make Oliver Hill's 1933 Dorland Hall boudoir seem plain.[39] The end wall was clad in black Vitrolite, with a large mural by Pollitzer sandblasted into the glazing, and then treated with silver bronze.[40] Other surfaces were clad in pink cathedral glass, the floor was in green Vitrolite, and the fireplace was made up of sheets of glass laid horizontally to form a series of exposed veneers. Pollitzer's decoration was on a silvered polished plate with the designs deeply sandblasted into the face. Every technique, process and finish was proudly set out. This was not about mass-market production or bringing quality design to the masses; on the contrary, it was 'high end', very expensive and bespoke, having limited application and appeal beyond exclusive residential projects and cruise ships.[41]

Despite this exclusivity, the interior spaces were very much a showcase of Pilkington's highly advanced materials and imaginative installations, whereas the exterior form and materiality was more conventional, probably to meet the rapid construction times demanded. Rowse again adopted masonry as the main facing material, which he sculpted into a sleek clock-tower beacon, with the intention of displaying the company name in large vertically orientated Vitrolite lettering.

Sheetworks showroom with decoration by K Cheeseman and S Pollitzer

The projecting curved tower, again inspired by Dutch modernism, was a means of creating a distinctive building, adding mass and increasing the scale in a relatively inexpensive manner. Rather like the curved staircase motif at the Philharmonic Hall, it softened the crisp edges of the large blocks behind and also highlighted the entrance beneath the cantilevered canopy.

The use of brick rather than glass was somewhat surprising, especially as Pollitzer noted that Pilkington 'exercised no design restraint on my design suggestions' and there is no reason to suggest they would have done with Rowse either.[42] This isn't to say his design was flawed or compromised – the circular-drum, horse-shoe arrangement and upward thrust of the tower all make for a very pleasing composition and refined ensemble of forms – there is just a nagging question of what could have been if Rowse had ventured into the territory of glazed façades. He was certainly technically competent and adventurous enough to design such a solution, as his experience in cantilevered steel-framed structures in Liverpool demonstrate. However, he remained steadfast in his view of façades as solid surfaces to be punched with fenestration, and he doubted whether glazed façades would achieve the necessary level of insulation. Glass façades were also at that time not integrated or resolved 'kits', but rather prototype installations requiring considerable detailing and abutment of various products and systems.[43] The Peter Jones department store was a piecemeal fabrication of a variety of uncoordinated components that did not result in quicker or simpler construction;[44] Rowse would not want to engage with this level of risk, and nor would Pilkington, who were eager for suitable accommodation rather than turning their own headquarters into a working laboratory.

Among the heavy plant and factory works of St Helens, Rowse plumped for a solution that would resist the environmental demands as well as possess enough fortitude to nestle within the gritty, industrial context. Again, in homage to John Hughes, the curved and sweeping façades contrast with the spikey saw-tooth roofs of the workshops and bland utilitarian repetition of the factory fenestration. The old head office looked like part of the works – a large shed housing rows of clerks, with the management in domestic-like properties – whereas the new build was in stark contrast to this. The three bands of brickwork with ribbon windows sandwiched between offered a refined approach: efficient, controlled and forward looking without being heretical. It was a move from a ramshackle workshop filled with furnaces and tinkering artisans to a modern, managed production line. New products, new management, new organisation, with the Victorian factory furnace aesthetic giving way to the smooth curve of the display cabinet filled with the latest products and materials. It was a business where they could model their products and turn the office into a working, but highly controlled, exhibition.

The horseshoe form resulted in curved interior spaces, breaking down the effect of long monotonous corridors while also creating a sense of expectation. The furniture in the directors' dining room adopted the same curvature of the façade, dampening the formality of a rectilinear dining arrangement (and reflecting the less hierarchical management?), while the bespoke carpet with wave motif was repeated on the exterior brick specials (a similar pattern was used on the Birkenhead tunnel extracts). Cheeseman designed the 10m-long conference table entirely out of glass, embodying a metal heating element so that the table was warm to the touch. Edward Carter Preston (1885–1965), a student contemporary of Rowse at Liverpool University's 'Art Sheds', designed glass panels for the visitors' lunch room to contrast with the veneered walnut walls and to exhibit various techniques, such as brilliant-cutting, acid-embossing and so on.[45]

The industrialised landscape of of St Helens

Rowse would have welcomed these interventions and the collaborative nature of working with innovative artists and specialist fabricators. All of his major commissions relied on the integration of building and sculpture to enliven the façades, to tell stories, and more broadly to act as a civic or community gesture. The architecture was unadorned and restrained, but this did not negate the desire for sculpture and applied decoration. If anything, it allowed the architecture to serve as a vehicle for artistic intervention. These buildings were seen not merely as a utilitarian device to serve the clients' needs (although this was always addressed) but also as a creative place for explorative and cultural advancement through an alliance with artists. When discussing the general approach of the Glasgow Empire Exhibition (where Rowse designed the United Kingdom Pavilion), Reilly also commented on this necessity for artistic collaboration: 'The modern plain, mainly rectangular, architecture calls out for both [sculpture and fresco]. There must be some relief to its bald truthfulness. Human nature cannot live on such rarefied, abstract stuff alone'.[46]

In addition to this artistic embellishment of architecture, the increased complexity and technical requirements of materials such as glass and its multiple applications and processes saw the creation of 'design service departments' being offered by the major manufacturers, including Pilkington.

Cheeseman explained that 'the architect must no longer insist on personally designing every piece of furniture and every fitting in his building, but must be content, so far as the interior finishing is concerned, to be a co-ordinator only – leaving the actual detailing of the more functional features to those who specialise, and are constantly in touch with the many technical processes involved.'[47] While Rowse may have baulked at being labelled a 'co-ordinator', the ability to collaborate and experiment with other specialists, artisans and technicians was an approach he keenly pursued.

School of Pharmacy

When the Queen Mother opened the new School of Pharmacy at University of London in April 1960, she described it as 'the oldest new building in London'. Whoever wrote her speech was spot on: between its commissioning in 1935 and the formal opening ceremony, 25 years had come and gone. It was at once Herbert Rowse's first major London commission and his last completed building before his death in 1963. Success in securing the commission encouraged him to think in terms of a breakthrough into London's building world and he may even have opened a small London office, because the box on his 1937 Pharmacy Society plan describes him as 'Herbert J Rowse FRIBA, Architect, Liverpool and London'. World War II frustrated any such ambitions by halting

Headquarters for the Pharmacy Society and later the Pharmacy School at UCL, known as the Pharmacy Building

work in 1940 on what was then still a half-built project for the Pharmaceutical Society headquarters and school. The latter was recognised for many years by the University of London for the award of degrees and the appointment of professors and other academic staff, but it was run entirely by the Society until 1949.

The construction stand-still was to last some 14 years. The architectural journals carried stories in 1947 and 1948 anticipating an imminent renewal of building work; however, post-war construction costs, building controls and the Society's financial difficulties finally forced the client to abandon the dream.[48] The incomplete building was sold in 1949 to the University of London, which had effectively taken over the year before.[49] During the war, the incomplete building had been weatherproofed and used as a depository for furniture and valuables salvaged from bomb-damaged houses. After the University's acquisition of the site, there was further delay until, in 1954, work was resumed on what was by then a remodelled scheme. Progressive fitting out and occupation of the building, floor by floor, finally reached completion in 1959, and the opening ceremony took place the following year, in a building that had been partly occupied for some years.

The original objective was for a formal Central London presence for the Society in a complex building that would provide club facilities, a publishing house, grand rooms (library, museum and assembly hall), public lecture theatre, academic teaching accommodation and research laboratories. The society's journal enthusiastically promised its members a London club close to a number of mainline stations as well as formal rooms for stylish social events. On the chosen architectural style itself, the statement in the *Pharmaceutical Journal* that followed the acceptance of Rowse's design stated:

> In the matter of form and architectural design, it has always been the Society's wish that their new home should be a building authentically belonging to its time, yet in its formal expression free from the eccentricities of fashionable experiments. It should have a general association with the collegiate tradition, and at the same time exhibit the character of a home for a professional body. The architect, Mr Rowse, has endeavoured to produce a building having its roots in a sound English tradition, at the same time utilising the diverse elements of the programme of requirements to produce an original scheme.[50]

Contemporary, but not eccentric; collegiate in a 'sound English tradition'. Some of these words would recur in other press releases from Rowse, but in this part of London, they were not merely formulaic. The setting was Georgian Bloomsbury, largely domestic in character to the east of Southampton Row and rising three or four storeys over basements. To the west, Charles Holden's gigantic stripped-classical scheme for the university Senate House and its library tower rose over Russell Square. The model used by the Society and its architect in cost comparisons just before the war was the rather earlier School of Hygiene and Tropical Medicine by Percy Morley Horder and Verner O Rees, completed in 1926, which employed Georgian proportions and a very regular overall form for an ashlar-faced steel-framed structure enclosing a similar mixture of research laboratories and collegiate facilities. Rowse chose brick cladding for what was going to be a taller and more highly modelled building in the brick environment of Brunswick Square.

The Society had decided early in the planning process to appoint an architect rather than go for a competition. In 1928, the Sub-Committee on Premises had acquired from the Foundling Hospital Estate 14 houses on the north side of Brunswick Square, one of which had been the home of members of the Bloomsbury Group. The Society's estate agents – George Lansdown & Brown – had also valued their Bloomsbury property and prepared a feasibility study and estimate for a new building costing £195,000 (including laboratory fixtures but not their apparatus). The surveyors may have hoped to be given the design project. However, at the meeting of the Sub-Committee on Premises, H H Linstead minuted,

> Appointment of an Architect – While there is much to be said for utilising the services of Messrs. Lansdown and Brown for certain of the work involved, the building will be such that an architect of experience in the erection of public and scientific buildings should be appointed for the general supervision of the work. It is possible to choose such an architect by competition, but I consider the deliberate selection of a suitable man will in the long run prove more satisfactory. This is the advice strongly given by officers of the University of London who had a similar and even more important selection to make.[51]

The Sub-Committee duly agreed: 'They propose to obtain names from various quarters and to select from the persons suggested, several from whom the final choice can be made after they have been interviewed and their work investigated.'[52] The Sub-Committee visited eight buildings (presumably by eight different architects) before shortlisting three, and at the Council Meeting in February 1935, recommended Herbert Rowse: 'a bold choice with purely Liverpool buildings to his name'.[53]

By the time Rowse's first plans were submitted in 1936, it was becoming clear that the Society's financial resources and construction prices were not even nearly matched. The sum of £200,000 had been budgeted following the feasibility study, but in October 1936, following concern over higher than expected cost estimates, a detailed comparison with the smaller School of Tropical Medicine suggested a likely overall cost of £350,000 for the seven floors of the Pharmacy building then envisaged.[54] The Sub-Committee on Premises recommended a number of cost saving options.[55] The roof-level refectory disappeared; the museum (which in the Society's new Dockland headquarters displays a magnificent collection of chemical instruments as well as artworks) was placed on the library gallery in the scheme accepted in February 1937.[56] But in 1936, the Society still enjoyed low interest rates, and had resolved to borrow until, in September 1937, the Treasurer drew attention to press reports of rapid increases in building costs, which had risen some 35 per cent in the 12 months to May 1937. Steel had risen 20 per cent in the 18 months to July 1937, and was expected to rise much faster as the re-armament programme got into its stride. Even allowing for the reductions made to the design, the Treasurer concluded that another £100,000 would be needed to complete the building.[57] Tenders were the acid test, and when these came in, Rowse was confronted with a request to achieve an additional £50,000 of savings.[58] After a meeting in September 1938, Rowse was charged with finding cuts of £40,000 to £45,000.[59] It is not reported how, or even if, this was achieved.

By early December 1938, the site excavation was about to commence, and the Society increasingly focused on nationwide funding efforts.[60] 'Will England match the Welsh?' asked the editors, reporting the efforts of the Wales branches, motivated by a promise to 'identify the principality with one of the rooms in our new home'.[61] Another two years would be needed before completion, but 'patience will be rewarded by a property of which every member will be proud to know that he is part-owner; a place which he can use as a rendezvous or even as his London club'.[62] An important element in the Society's promotional campaign was the weekly publication of a journal column, 'Progress at Brunswick Square', which chronicled events on site, illustrating them with a mast-head that changed regularly to mark the work of the demolition contractors, the removal of the spoil heap from the foundations and basement, the appearance of site cranes and then the steel frame in April 1939.[63]

The 'Progress' column picked up on the growing threat of war. 'Now that a Minister of Supply has been appointed, supplies of steel for purposes of rearmament may be curtailed, but there will be no interference with the plans for our new headquarters', because, following the advice of Rowse, steel was even now being delivered and stockpiled on site.[64] Work slowed after the outbreak of war because of the call-up of labour, and delay – rather than abandonment – was anticipated.[65] The last entry, in January 1940, was determinedly optimistic: 'There is no room for doubt that it [our building] will be a landmark in the district and this, not because of any bizarre feature but rather on account of the expanse of its notable façade distinguished by architectural embellishments at once unusual and yet subdued and dignified'.[66]

The incomplete structure of 1940 was weatherproofed for what turned out to be a lengthy hiatus. Four floors and a basement had been completed, with the uppermost structural frame just visible over the fifth-floor façade. Windows and screeds – but few of the internal finishes – were in place for the completed floors.[67]

When Rowse was recalled after the War by the University of London to complete their new building, a number of significant changes were implemented, but the key formal features of the design remained almost untouched.

Then and now, the prominent main entrance on the long front façade facing Brunswick Square leads into an elegant Art Deco entrance lobby, from which the grand public rooms open. To the right, a flat-floor hall features a small stage capable of handling drama or serving as a podium for speeches. Originally, the society's library was to have been to the left, with alcoves under a gallery. In the remodelled scheme, the library was replaced by a traditional college-style refectory with long tables and bench seating, a raised dais for the staff high table, and a selection of exhibits from the library in show cases along the gallery wall (where the reduced museum of the pre-war scheme would have been displayed).

Pharmacy Building: interior perspective watercolour showing the proposed library

Straight ahead, the entrance lobby leads directly to a tiered lecture hall, with the raked overhang covering an inquiry (or ticket) desk and cloakrooms. In the pre-war scheme, the Society's council chamber had been above the lecture hall. This area survives as the school's main committee room (the school first a college of London University, now part of a much-enlarged University College). The freestanding lecture-hall complex rose for three floors from basement to first-floor level in an almost separate block, flanked on each side by open courtyards.

In the 1937 scheme, the spaces off the entrance lobby were to have formed the formal face of the Society. Academic staff and students had a separate entrance on the right (east) end of the main façade, which served an office suite, meeting room, senior common room and small teaching lab and lecture theatre.

Pharmacy Building refectory

Members of the Society had another small entrance at the left (west) corner, with cloakrooms, a club room and offices as well as space for the Society's publishing efforts. The upper floors on the main façade were occupied by the much larger research labs, with the animal houses on the roof, where the spectacular refectory had been imagined.

The main entrance and school doorway still serve something close to their original purpose. What would have been the former members' premises in the west wing were replanned after the war to provide examination labs for the whole of London University (which, before microchemistry came in during the 1960s, involved extensive rows of benches with sinks and services connections for each exam candidate). The staff offices and research labs – much modernised – still occupy the main upper floors of the building – and have been expanded in a much more recent remodelling to fill the former open courtyards surrounding the major lecture theatre. Inside, one moves through formerly open space on a series of high-tech catwalks. The school library has moved to quarters in the rear of the east wing.

Rowse's challenge was to design what is – even in its slightly reduced form – a very large building, located in what was then still a dignified residential Georgian square. Set-backs in the section are explained as a product of daylighting regulations, but also meant that the bulk of the laboratories was broken up and concealed by the side wings, which projected to the building line and were themselves scaled to match the adjacent residential façade lines. The front (south) façade to the square was too big for this to work, particularly when seen from right across the square, a view that tended to flatten the set-backs. Nor could Rowse simply replicate the Georgian piano nobile, because the grand rooms with their tall windows were all on the ground floor. Rowse kept them as the dominant feature, playing with the fenestration of the upper floors with a ribbon window, and separating it from the tall ground-floor windows by a series of square openings. The main (south) façade was punctuated by the vertical staircase towers marking the side doors.

The grand public rooms that the Society planned as the public face of the pharmaceutical profession and its social life had been completed (but not finished or decorated) before the long standstill. However, a number of original colour perspectives preserved in the school's library show interior designs (dated 1959) for the entrance lobby and the large spaces opening off it. Rowse's taste for rich polychromatic interior design had clearly not dimmed. More surprisingly, perhaps, the university and UCL bought into this image and have retained it through the inevitable schemes of modernisation and internal remodelling. The school's refectory – originally to have been the society's library – retains an appropriately collegiate atmosphere and something of Rowse's very personal ability to combine modern design and technology with rich historical borrowings.

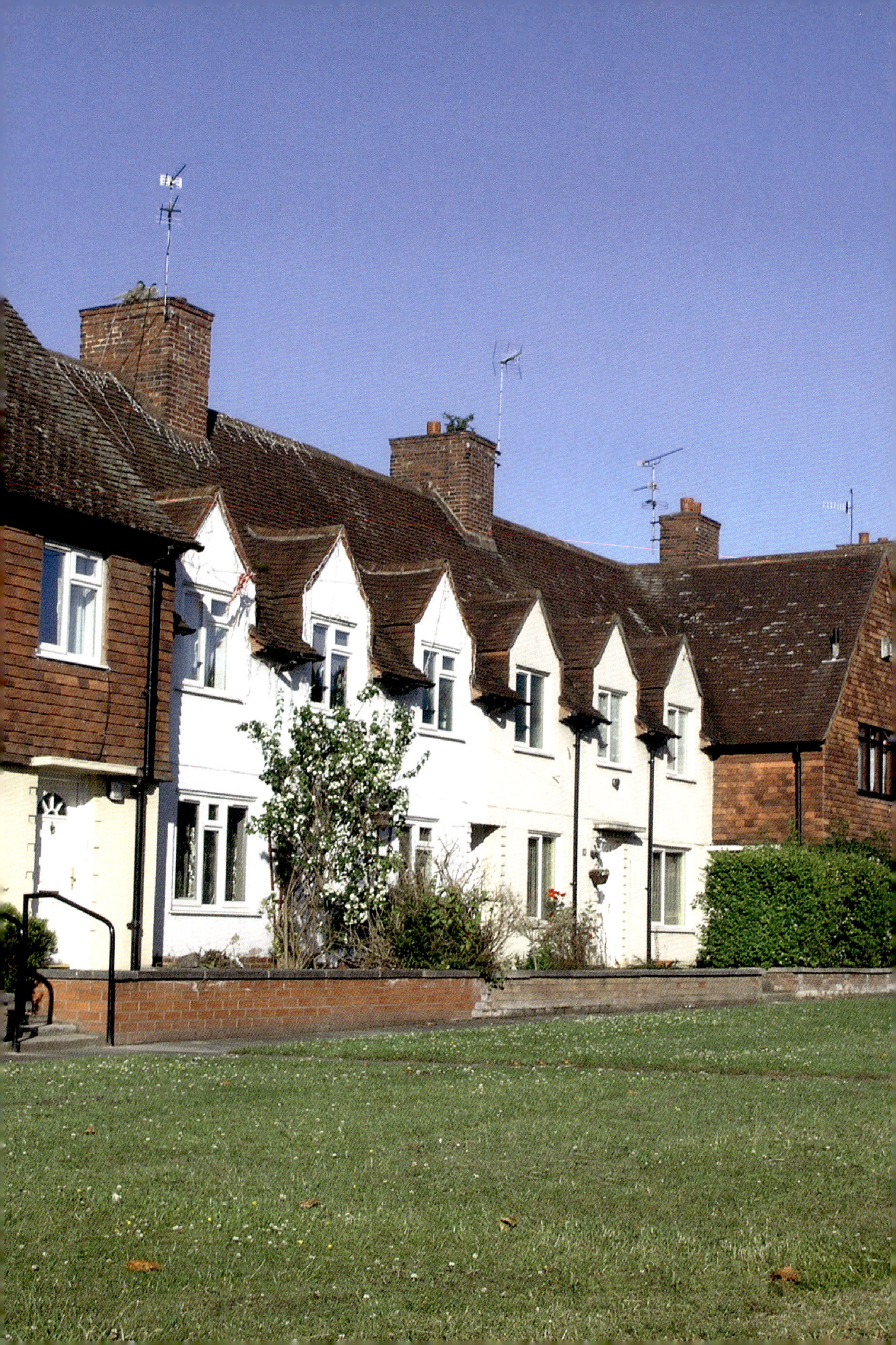

5 Social housing and planning

More than once in his career Herbert Rowse tackled the design of the social housing that was to become such a feature of the 20th century. In 1912, he and Sydney Kelly were commended for their entry to a competition for the Prestatyn Estate, North Wales.[1] The competition was for the layout of what amounted to a small Garden City, rather than the dwellings themselves. It had been promoted by Lord Aberconway and the Trustees of the Prestatyn Estate, property of the Pochin family of Manchester, into which Aberconway (the barrister and former Liberal MP Charles McLaren) had married. He also commissioned Rowse, after World War I, to build 600 miners' houses at Rainhill, just outside St Helens, Aberconway being chairman of the nearby Sutton Heath and Lea Green collieries. Like most such colliery housing, it employed two-storey cottages built in short terraces and staggered to make interesting street views. The scheme was published by Charles Reilly, who praised its neo-Georgian details, which the professor saw as 'much nearer the new standard of civilization to which it was hoped to raise the working-class dwellings, than most of the similar houses since built'.[2] Yet until the early 1930s, the opportunity to design housing for a local authority had eluded Rowse. His work on Birkenhead's tunnel entrances, however, caught the eye of Alderman Denis Clarke, the Birkenhead-appointed Deputy Chairman of the Merseyside Tunnel Joint Committee. Clarke invited Rowse to offer his services to Birkenhead's Estates Committee when the town embarked upon the redevelopment of a site not far from the Georgian elegance of Hamilton Square.

Throughout the 1920s, central government housing subsidies had encouraged 'general needs' house building to produce new accommodation, nearly all of which took the form of low-density, low-rise suburban estates on greenfield sites. The Housing Act passed in 1930 by the Labour Government adjusted the subsidy system to finance the rehousing of people (often in large families) displaced by slum clearance.[3] By necessity, much of the rehousing continued to be built in the suburbs. Liverpool, almost uniquely among English cities outside London, also promoted an ambitious inner-city flat-building programme aimed, theoretically, at casually employed dock workers and others who needed to live close to their work (although in practice, such tenants were often unable to afford the higher rents charged for high-cost central flats). The blocks were generally five storeys high, and the flats reached by stairs and open-access galleries: later, improved designs gave interior-staircase access and bigger

Cottages at Woodchurch Estate

flats with sheltered balconies set into the block (and let at substantially higher rents). The new flats enjoyed an unusual degree of local all-party support on the Liverpool City Council, overcoming the Left's traditional opposition to multistorey solutions. Lancelot Keay, Liverpool's Director of Housing and later City Architect, quickly became one of Britain's leading advocates for flat-based redevelopment, hiring some of Reilly's best students to design the schemes using an explicitly Modernist vocabulary of brick and concrete, stripped of ornament, with sweeping horizontal lines, ribbon windows (or the appearance of such), sun balconies and (again, the illusion of) flat roofs. The blocks frequently wrapped around a sheltered central courtyard for relaxation, children's play, and laundry-drying racks. Liverpool's best-known scheme was St Andrews Gardens (often known as the Bullring for its horseshoe shape and because it replaced an abattoir). A perspective drawing from 1932 by John Hughes (one of 'Reilly's boys' working in Keay's department) captures very well the self-consciously Modern style for the walk-up tenements – decent enough by the standards of the time, but not fundamentally more advanced or progressive than the blocks built by London councils forced to adopt flatted solutions by land prices and the high pre-clearance densities of many slum sites.[4] It would be misleading to say that Liverpool built flats entirely because of their high visibility, and 'the exciting architectural potential of large central buildings … [allowing] local politicians [to] publicise their progress in events such as exhibitions and formal openings'.[5] But, as Newbery argued, this was certainly an important contributory factor. As we have seen with the tunnel structures, Liverpool and Birkenhead both placed a high value on architectural quality.

St Andrews Square flats, Camden Street, Birkenhead

Birkenhead also needed inner-area housing for those employed in the docks and shipbuilding yards, and in the early 1930s, initiated their own flat-building programme, starting with a site in the Camden Street area. In October 1931, the Borough Engineer submitted a sketch plan of the redevelopment.[6] It soon became clear that Birkenhead wanted something better looking than the Borough Engineer's Department could produce. The Estates Committee's invitation received a reply 'from Mr Herbert J Rowse, Architect, Liverpool (dated 11 February 1932) offering to submit a scheme of development of the Camden Street area with flats on the terms stated'.[7] A month later, the Committee met with Rowse and, 'after hearing the views of the committee, [Rowse] promised to prepare a scheme for submission to the committee at an early date'.[8] The Camden Street site for 68 flats and another tenement scheme of 24 flats would be used to rehouse some of those displaced by the clearance of properties in the St Mary's Gate Clearance Scheme, which combined slum clearance with the creation of a riverfront site for the future Tranmere graving docks. By October 1932, Rowse's proposal for blocks containing flats of three, four and five rooms on three sides of the site was provisionally approved, subject to cost assessment by the Borough Treasurer and negotiations with the Ministry of Health.[9] There was now no doubt about the role of the scheme as a showpiece for Birkenhead. Alderman Van Gruisen, Chairman of the Estates Committee, described it as a 'Model Flats Scheme' and went on to report that the Committee

> was branching out on an improved type of flat for people who had been de-housed [by slum clearance]. They had secured a prominent site facing two main roads in the town, *and had therefore as fine an elevation point as possible* ... They had overcome some of the very ugly features of building flats without incurring any increase in cost.

Van Gruisan 'hoped it would be followed by further blocks of similar flats'.[10] By May 1933, the local press reported that a Joint Sub-committee of the Health and Estates Committees was considering a further programme of six blocks in the north, centre and south of the borough.[11] Rowse may have been forgiven for feeling optimistic about the prospect of a continuous stream of social-housing commissions from Birkenhead.

St Andrews Square: model flats for Birkenhead

Camden Street used four-storey, walk-up, gallery-access blocks, containing mainly two- and three-bedroom flats and a few larger units. Three brick-faced blocks enclosed a triangular island site bounded by Camden Street, Conway Street and Claughton Road (all now beneath Birkenhead's central shopping centre car park, together with St Andrews Church, which gave the scheme its name). Parabolic brick archways gave access to the courtyard with its playground and a 'covered space for perambulators and bicycles'. The projecting bullnose sun balconies were decorated with patterned brickwork, and a horizontal

St Andrews Square: parabolic arch entranceway

ribbon-window effect was achieved by introducing patterned darker-toned brickwork in the panels that separated the windows. Further decoration below the cornice and directly above the entranceway was modelled on the brickwork of the Mersey Tunnel ventilation towers. The shallow-pitched roofs were hidden from close-up view by a parapet, giving a clean finish to the blocks. *Building*'s coverage included cutaway isometric drawings to illustrate the constructional details, including the Truscon reinforced-concrete system for the floors, cantilevered balconies and galleries (a system used on a scheme jointly developed a few years later by Truscon and Lancelot Keay's design team, featuring 10-storey cylindrical concrete blocks, which was published but never built).[12] 'Nautilus flues' extracted air through horizontal ceiling ducts and vertical flues concealed in the back of the fitted kitchen cupboards. Ventilation was a problem in the heavily polluted inner districts of Birkenhead, and tenants were notoriously unwilling to leave windows open in gallery-access blocks.

By early 1935, the almost completed project was in difficulty, work at a standstill and the contractor evidently going into bankruptcy.[13] After delays while the contract was reassigned, Rowse informed the Committee on 13 June that the first group of flats would be ready for occupation on 19 June, and invited members to visit them before the tenants moved in. The Committee visited the Camden Street flats on 17 June, afterwards viewing the tenements on New Chester Road.[14] There was no grand opening ceremony, no further publicity and no more public-sector commissions for Herbert Rowse from Birkenhead. This had much to do with changing political fortunes in the town.

The changing political context for housing in Birkenhead

While the Camden Street flats were taking shape, the council had been forced to defend its plans for the Woodchurch Estate, a tract of largely undeveloped land that had been absorbed into Birkenhead by boundary changes and purchased in 1926.[15] A plan for Woodchurch had been prepared by Thomas H Mawson (1861–1933), a well-known landscape designer, President of the Town Planning Institute and frequent lecturer in Civic Design at the University of Liverpool. Mawson had undertaken considerable work for Lord Leverhulme, designing the landscaping at Thornton Manor and parts of Port Sunlight.[16] His design was more of a strategic overview of how Arrowe Park, Landican and Woodchurch might alleviate the problems of an increasingly congested Birkenhead. Arrowe Park and its mansion house were to be retained as parkland and a golf links; Landican was to house a cemetery and crematorium; the ancient village of Woodchurch was to be the site of a large new housing estate. The road layout was modelled loosely on Port Sunlight, and two small shopping areas were stipulated, but detailed housing layouts were not provided at this stage. The plan lay dormant for around five years, when it was revised by Mawson's son, Edward Prentice Mawson (1885–1954), to show houses for sale using 999-year building leases.

Mawson plan for Woodchurch, Arrowe and Landican, 1927

Mawson plan for Woodchurch, 1944

Birkenhead's Labour councillors objected, arguing that the council should be building for rent.[17] There was a small amount of social housing shown on the plan with a bold red outline, but it was a token gesture. Other features also came under attack, such as the lack of provision for adult games (no space for football, cricket or even bowls) and without the swimming pool (or lido), which was becoming a feature of enlightened local-authority provision at this time.[18] This criticism followed what the Birkenhead News had described as an 'election landslide', which in November 1933, had seen Labour seize four council seats from the Conservatives, plus another gain when a member crossed the floor.[19] Control still lay with the Conservatives, but only just.

The newly appointed Borough Surveyor, Bertie Robinson, was instructed to pursue an overcrowding survey (in collaboration with the Medical Officer of Health), the tenement-building programme for rehoused slum dwellers described above, and to plan feeder roads and sewers and the plotting for private housing on the council-owned land at Woodchurch. The Labour group on council protested yet again.[20] But on this point, Labour was out-voted. The Birkenhead Conservatives put their faith in the private sector as providers of mass housing, taking advantage of a government scheme that allowed councils to borrow money cheaply from the Public Works Loan Board and then to relend it as 'local authority mortgages', while using its own powers to assemble sites. Woodchurch, as we shall see, remained under grass until after World War II.

What marked the temporary banishment of Rowse from Birkenhead was a spat that enlivened the council meeting following the close-run November 1933 local elections. A special committee report on the reorganisation of the Borough Engineer and Surveyor's Department stressed the heavy workload, increased staff and shortage of accommodation in a department struggling to cope with a massive increase in the size of the borough. New office accommodation was recommended, and Alderman Denis Clarke (the Conservative Chairman of the Finance Committee) told the council that a new municipal annexe was proposed for a site adjacent to the Town Hall on Hamilton Square. Clarke told the meeting that 'It was proposed to engage Mr Rowse, because it was necessary in this case to have a building which would be most pleasing to the town and in keeping with the architecture of Hamilton Square'.[21] This did not go down well. The Birkenhead News described the subsequent exchanges as 'breezy'.

William Egan, Leader of the Labour councillors, opposed Rowse's appointment, arguing that Mr Rowse would not have been in contention without the 'personal feeling' of Alderman Clarke. Rowse had won 'some favour' as architect of the ventilation stations, but the 'out of the ordinary' flats in Camden Street had had to be redesigned to get within Ministry cost limits. Furthermore, the Corporation had its own salaried architects, 'and yet denied to these men the right to design a Corporation building. Outside architects also were asking

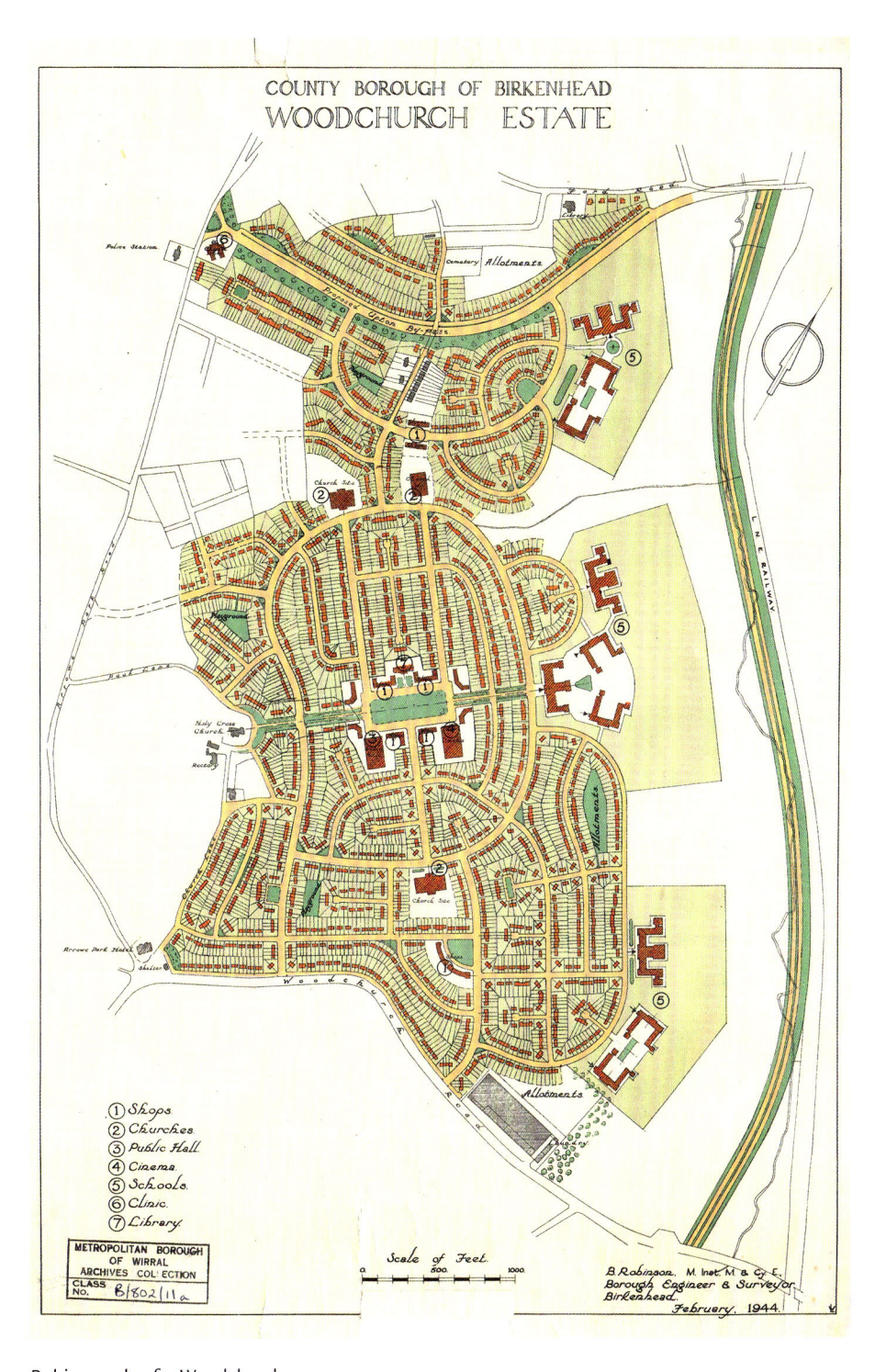

Robinson plan for Woodchurch

whether all of the Corporation work was going to one man'. In reply, Alderman Clarke 'accepted that his admiration for Mr Rowse knew no bounds. He induced Mr Rowse to put in for the buildings, and when they were put up he was sure the town would be proud of them.' Clarke went on to contend that the Corporation-designed flats in St Mary's Gate were a cheap and shoddy job and were creating slums.[22] There were clearly local frustrations and jealousies, and these would resurface embarrassingly a few years later when the Borough Engineer's plans for Woodchurch were very publicly criticised by Charles Reilly. Any remaining prospects of a commission for the Town Hall extension died when Alderman Clarke himself died in September 1934. A year later, Egan became leader of the council, this time with a knife-edge Labour majority. The Conservatives regained control of Birkenhead in 1938 and remained in control throughout the war, with many crises to meet, but without the ability to achieve anything in housing beyond planning for a post-war future. At this point, Professor Reilly re-enters the story.

Reilly's Birkenhead Plan and the Woodchurch controversy

Rowse's commission in 1944 to redesign the Woodchurch housing estate – eventually delivering one of the more original low-rise housing projects to be built in the post-war years – came in the aftermath of a chaotic series of events that followed the appointment of Reilly to undertake a reconstruction plan for Birkenhead.

The immediate background to the Birkenhead plan was, as in many other British towns, extensive war damage, a legacy of slums, the many Government promises made during the war for a post-war house-building campaign and – not to be overlooked – a widespread belief in planning itself. The most famous of the wartime plans, the *County of London Plan* by John Forshaw (the LCC Chief Architect) and Patrick Abercrombie (by then a Professor of Town Planning at University College London and Consultant to the LCC) was published at the beginning of July 1943, to a fanfare of national publicity. July 1943 also saw the first proposals by Birkenhead councillors for a reconstruction and development plan, coupled with a proposal to appoint a city architect, who was to be qualified both as an architect and a town planner.[23] Consideration of the proposal for a Borough Architect was deferred by Council to 27 October 1943, and postponed again to 3 November 1943, when by amendment, it was decided not to appoint an architect but instead to obtain the services of the 'best expert or experts opinion' on the future shape of Birkenhead.[24] The former head of the Liverpool School of Architecture seemed like the perfect choice.[25] Professor Reilly, retired since 1936 and 70 years old when commissioned, was still one of the most authoritative voices in architecture, plus he had good knowledge of the region and time to work on the plan. During the war, he had busied himself writing a veritable stream of newspaper and journal articles on what would be needed after victory. Still a larger-than-life contrarian, and driven by fierce enthusiasms for the latest idea, Reilly was now 'an old man in a hurry'. Despite failing health, he was very excited by the prospect of a new urban architecture replacing wartime ruins, and an advocate of Soviet-style 'shock troops' of architects who would deliver the reconstruction of Britain.[26] His latest idea was 'community planning'.[27] Not only should housing estates be equipped with the local shops and social facilities so often sadly lacking in inter-war schemes, but the traditional forms of council developments borrowed from the garden suburbs needed to be fundamentally rethought, exchanging large private gardens for something closer to the 'traditional' English village green. A shared open space would become the new focus for the community. To win space for the greens, the low-density wide-fronted (often semi-detached) house types of the inter-war years would be replaced by narrow-fronted modern terraces with very small private yards. A similarly conceived but much higher-density scheme would be proposed for the inner residential areas of Birkenhead, again based on communal open space. Before Reilly had been commissioned, however, the largest tract of house-building land already owned by Birkenhead had been planned by the staff of the Borough Engineer, Bertie Robinson. (Indeed, it was planned before the war and replanned more than once during it.)

Reilly stumbled across Robinson's plan for Woodchurch while visiting the Engineer's offices in connection with his Birkenhead proposals. Robinson's team had proposed a standard low-density suburban solution featuring semi-detached houses with large gardens – which by 1944 had been fully 10 years in the making. Reilly deemed it a 'damn bad plan' and offered to collaborate with Robinson to remake it. Not surprisingly Reilly's criticism and offer of 'help' was much resented by the Council's building professionals. It was resented, too, by the Conservative controlling group (who had appointed Reilly) when the Labour opposition took up Reilly's cause, calling for a redesign on the community open-space principles advocated by the Professor.[28] Reilly denigrated the Robinson plan as 'isolationist', claiming that there would be no community spirit or sense of collective belonging. He sought to 'retain the friendliness of the little streets and slums' through the shared greens and clubhouses.[29] Labour support prompted a well-reported public meeting and a vote, which came out in favour of the Reilly scheme with its vision of community interaction and space for sports, lectures and film nights.[30] *The Tribune* even summoned up and weaponised the 'community spirit [that] came to the fore in the blitz days. It appears the Tories don't like it'.[31] A national press campaign culminated in a feature article in *Picture Post* by the war correspondent Maurice Edelman, calling the affair 'The Battle of the Plans' and presenting it as a key engagement in the wider campaign for the planning of post-war Britain on modern lines. Birkenhead Council finally agreed to review their design for Woodchurch.[32]

Reilly's alternative had only ever been a rough sketch, overlaid on the Borough Engineer's plan and drawn freehand by the Professor overnight, as he himself relates in the foreword to Lawrence Wolfe's *The Reilly Plan*. This was a slim, somewhat sycophantic volume published in September 1945 by a left-wing sociologist who had become an evangelist for Reilly's social theories and hoped to stimulate interest in them among ministers in Clement Attlee's post-war government.[33] Reilly's sketch – and the Engineer's plan – had been tidied up and turned into bird's-eye views by *Picture Post*, and presented side-by-side across a double opening, together with photographs of Bertie Robinson and the Professor. But the *Picture Post* view still fell far short of a fully resolved alternative plan.[34]

Instead of working for the good of the borough, Reilly had stoked controversy and undermined confidence in the Chief Engineer. Birkenhead Council extracted an apology for his extraordinary behaviour. They could not sack him because the Council wanted the reconstruction plan, now behind schedule.

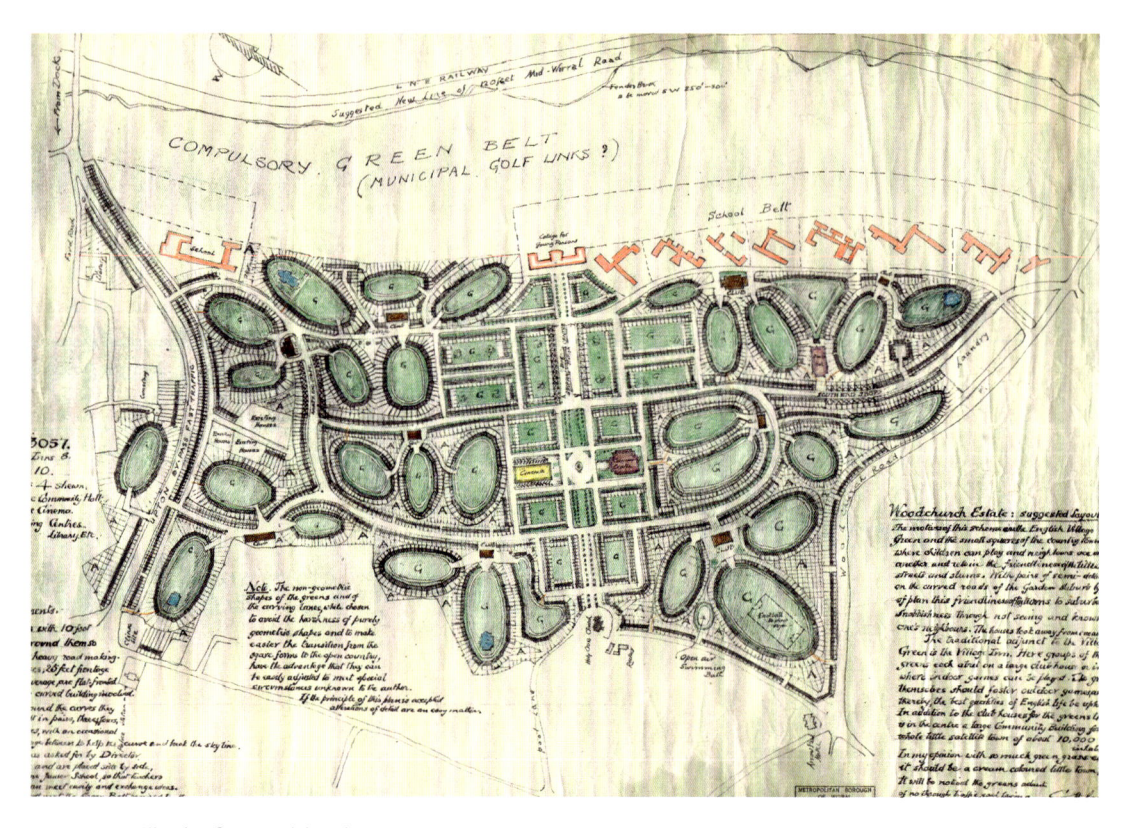

Reilly plan for Woodchurch

SOCIAL HOUSING AND PLANNING

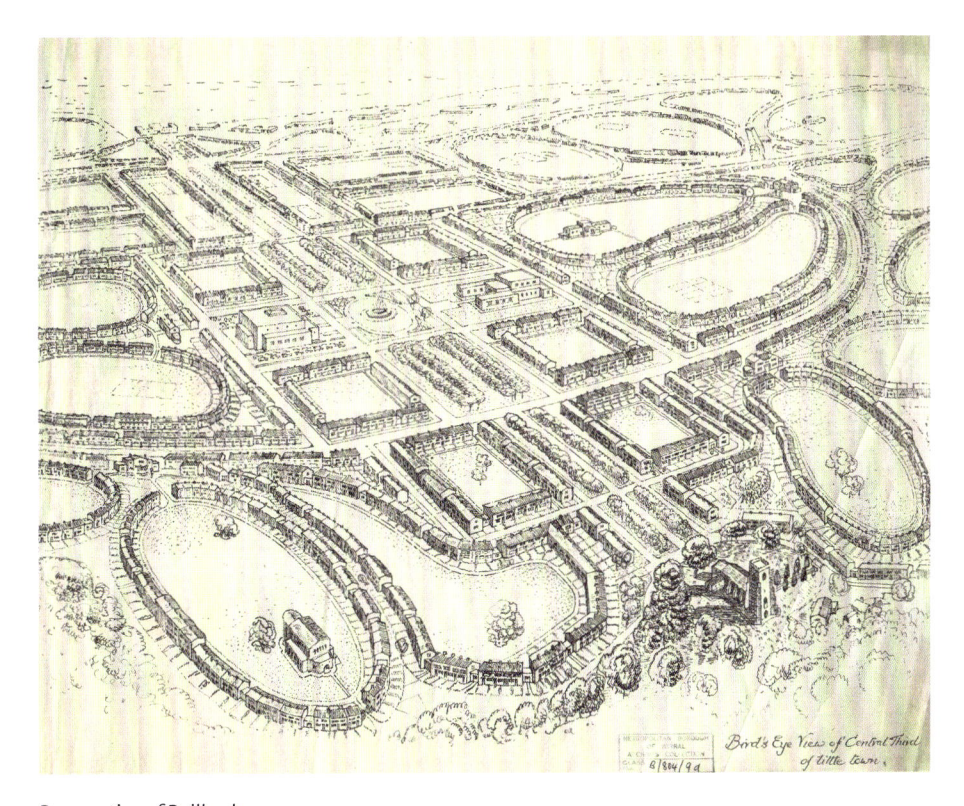

Perspective of Reilly plan

Moreover, Reilly had recently been knighted and awarded the Royal Gold Medal for Architecture, making it difficult to remove him without major public embarrassment. However, Birkenhead clearly were not now going to employ the Professor as their housing architect. Instead, the RIBA was asked to nominate a local architect to prepare new housing designs. The RIBA replied within days, recommending Herbert Rowse.[35] When Rowse re-entered the Birkenhead arena in September 1944, it was in the unlikely guise of peacemaker.[36]

Rowse and the Woodchurch compromise

> Alderman Prentice said the Rowse plan would mark an epoch in the history of Birkenhead; it was really artistic and practical. It covered 480 acres and provided for 2,500 houses; nearly half of the estate was devoted to open spaces. That was a feature which had never been included in any plan of this neighbourhood. There were ten houses to the acre … the gardens were three to four times the size of those in the Reilly plan. The people of Birkenhead never had such an opportunity offered to them; as a matter of fact, very few towns had an opportunity of developing an estate on the lines proposed by Mr. Rowse. It showed the hand of the real master.[37]

The *Birkenhead News* originally reported Rowse's Woodchurch commission as one to 'design the houses'. This seems to have been strictly accurate, but Rowse produced yet another master plan for Woodchurch, which, although also uninvited, seemed to temper the highly politicised debates and take the best features from both proposals. Rowse had to push Birkenhead Council to accept that house *qua* house design was not the real problem at Woodchurch, and that the concerns raised by the 'Battle of the Plans' would not be resolved without revisiting the wider layout, and attempting to salvage something of Reilly's ideas within an estate plan for which contracts for the early infrastructure and road layouts had already been made. Some of these had to be renegotiated. Redesign within the constraints of a partly settled estate layout was a formidable challenge for someone of Rowse's strong views. He probably only undertook the commission in a spirit of national service in wartime and,

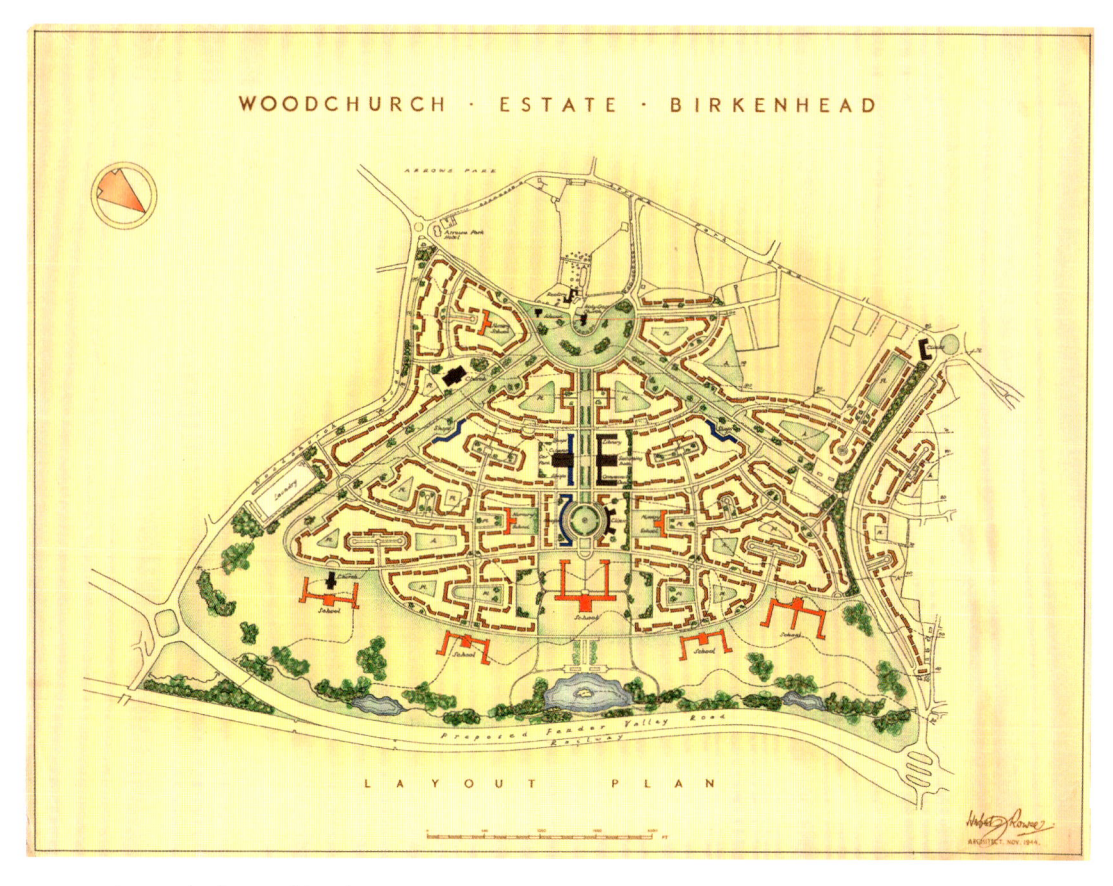

Rowse plan for Woodchurch

perhaps, a wish to assist an old man who had helped him at various times in his own career (and would not live to see the results of his manoeuvring).

Rowse's development, like that of the Borough Engineer, was planned as a self-contained neighbourhood in an overall scheme originally for 2,500 homes. The layout was formal, with a central avenue along which shops, clinics, a community centre, baths and library were sited. Schools were distributed around the edges of the housing, separated from main roads by a broad strip of parkland. The old village church, rectory and historic school were preserved as the focal point for the three main converging streets. Rowse's dwelling plans were for two-storeyed terraced-house types, a mixture of the normal one-room-plus-passageway frontages and the two-room-wide frontages widely used in inter-war housing (both public and private), rather than the very narrow-fronted types that had been proposed but never properly planned by Reilly.[38]

Cottage housing in Woodchurch

Strong axis leading towards the historic church and flanked on either side with housing

Housing types and open front gardens

The terraced blocks were composed to capture some of the qualities of traditional English village housing, gable-ended but with a variety of roof pitches, dormers and facing materials, and small set-backs to add interest to the street façades. There were no 'backs' as such to the houses, as all pipes and services were concealed, and the same quality materials used. The Corporation also agreed to Rowse's request to hide all telephone cables in underground ducts (at a cost of £16,000) to maintain an uncluttered feel to the streets,[39] as well as his consolidation of the road layout, which saved £20,000.[40] The bedroom floors were of concrete, saving timber and reducing the overall height of the houses, all 'watched with great interest by the Ministries concerned'.[41] The street frontages were 'open' in the American style – that is without small fenced-off front gardens – and the plot sizes had been manipulated to give somewhat smaller back gardens than those in the Borough Engineer's proposal, leaving room for shared common spaces between the blocks, linked together with pathways. The community spaces could be used as play areas, but provided nothing on the scale of the village greens suggested by the artist's impressions of the Reilly Plan (which had waxed enthusiastically on the cricket that could be played on them) or the published version of the Birkenhead Plan, which eventually appeared in 1947.[42] It was a compromise. Rowse's compromise, however, was among the first group of 35 post-war UK social housing schemes to be awarded the Minister of Health's housing medal in September 1950. Professor Gordon Stephenson, commenting on them for the *Architects' Journal*, reminded readers that

> Herbert Rowse's scheme at Woodchurch results from the famous Reilly-Borough Engineer fracas. Though Reilly himself did not design the neighbourhood, he was instrumental in having an architect do the job; and what more natural than that the architect was one of his famous students. The scheme, now only partly completed, is a curious combination of charming traditional cottages (expensive looking) and a layout which is monumental in its main lines of three converging roads with extraordinarily wide verges, but it is varied in detail.[43]

In a group of 60 houses, there could be as many as ten housing types: small variations and adjustments introduced variety without incoherence. In typical Rowse style, the outhouses were adjusted to suit the different scales of the houses. Unlike Reilly's scheme, where the houses faced onto a green, Rowse inverted this approach, using smaller grassed areas accessed from the rear gardens. This prevented the 'overlooked' element found in bye-law streets and created private enclosures for groups of houses. Children would be far safer playing here than running free on Reilly's larger greens out front.

Woodchurch housing and generous village green spaces

Steep pitches, dormers and chimneys to create the 'village ideal'

There is a strong sense that Rowse was trying to create a new Port Sunlight, but one with more architectural unity than Lever's 'one of everything' approach. As Lillian Potter notes in her doctoral study of the estate, 'the picturesque quality of the terraces of houses belies the reality that they are part of an extensive municipal estate'.[44] The strong axes shown in the plan were somewhat lost without the larger buildings lining the central vista; the smaller houses that were built there seem out of place, and allow the sight lines to disperse, rendering the long axis somewhat hollow, without a focal point or sense of enclosure. This was partially addressed when the dramatic Catholic church was bravely constructed at the end of the main axis, giving the axis a purpose and contrasting the old church facing it at the other end.

Despite the quality of the houses, the estate was considered out of step with other national developments pursued in the famous 'mixed developments' pioneered at Roehampton and Harlow. Potter pondered whether Woodchurch was sufficiently innovative 'to compete with the new style of development including flats and maisonettes, the typical features of later post-war planning'.[45] Rowse was clearly not averse to flats, but thought their place was in the towns rather than on the edge of the agricultural greenbelt.

Rowse's last task for Birkenhead Council was to provide designs for a formal entry to Woodchurch to celebrate the Queen's coronation. He resigned quite suddenly shortly afterwards, and other hands completed the later phases, which, sadly, included most of the promised social facilities that had been planned along the wide central avenue. Birkenhead had finally appointed a Borough Architect, T A Brittain, who was eager for his new department to make its mark. By 1955, two-storey flats were being built, followed by four-storey maisonettes in 1958.[46] The town's first 14-storey high-rise flats followed soon after, and achieved a notoriety comparable to that of the original 'Battle of the Plans' schemes when two blocks – Oak and Eldon Gardens – became the first post-war high-rise blocks to be demolished. The central part of the estate had by then deteriorated socially, climaxing in 1981, when two suicides and a small-scale riot (coinciding with the much more widespread disturbances in Toxteth) focused political attention once more on the area.[47]

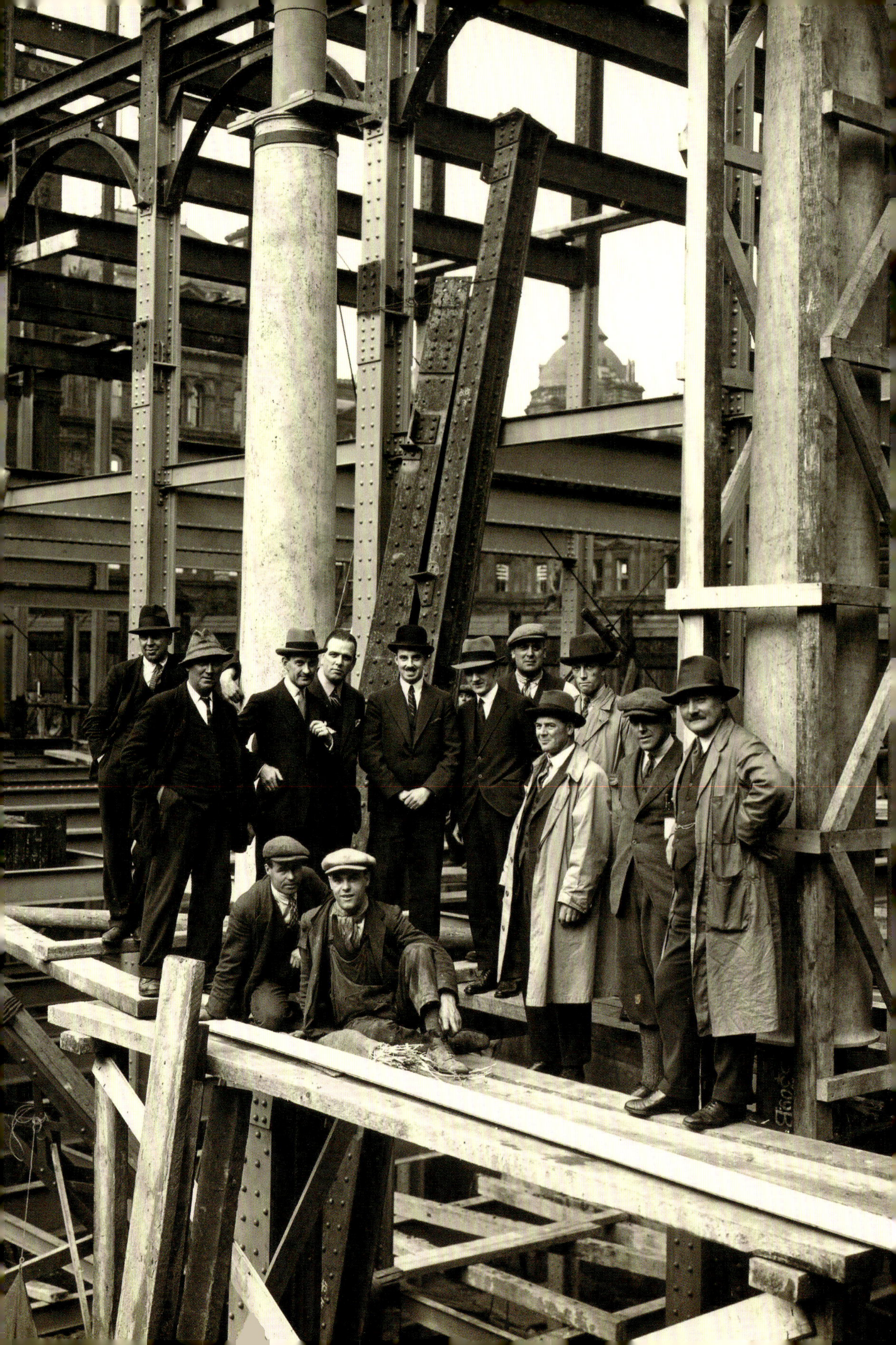

6 Conclusion

Rowse's career spanned almost five decades and covered some of the most turbulent periods of modern times. Operating at these moments of political upheaval, wars and economic crashes, Rowse delivered an extraordinary set of buildings across an array of building types. Specialisation was not an option from a business perspective, but equally, in creative terms, Rowse sought out the challenge of designing across many sectors with varied programmes. The factory, hospital, theatre, office, bank, school, villa, housing estate and tunnel extract were all confidently pursued, and seen as creative questions to answer. New problems were treated with a period of uninterrupted work until a refined solution was configured, and from a planning perspective, there is not a single Rowse project that is not fully resolved or that accepts compromise.

The interior and exterior were two very different enquiries for Rowse. The interior, certainly for the larger projects, was generally seen in terms of grand volumes treated with opulent and even extravagant materials. It was to be a place of drama, a theatrical encounter of different scenes, carefully choreographed and manipulated, with all structure and services concealed, or transformed into sculptural effect. The exterior was more usually aloof, generally of large monochromatic surfaces with occasional detailing and decoration. Walls were treated as solid, load-bearing elements, rather than a surface 'skin', and windows were pressed out from this hefty mass. Both interior and exterior components tended to be inspired by historical precedents, and Rowse maintained an extensive collection of sourcebooks, references and patterns that, to a large extent, informed his design approach. He was not looking to create a new architecture from scratch, but would heavily 'sample' and collage precedents to generate carefully composed solutions. Taking the role of a creative curator, he would arrange an assemblage of designs. Of course, these sources would be interpreted, translated, remade and adjusted to suit. The 'right' references would also need to be used, and Rowse was very much a 'taste maker' in this regard, with an eye for quality. He was not easily swayed by the latest fashions as presented in the journals of the day, and certainly had little appetite for trite Modernist revolution. Modernism did hold some appeal, however, when it was explored through the medium of brick. Brick was a staple material for Rowse, and he applied it confidently and eloquently, even on the massive ventilation towers, where it was masterfully used to convey human scale through its detailing as well as to wrap vast expanses without appearing bland.

Herbert Rowse (standing, third from left) with colleagues and contractors at Martins Bank

There was also a strong commitment to housing throughout Rowse's career – even when he had won substantial competitions, he still designed (or could not resist) small housing projects. He enjoyed working on the fundamental architectural question, that of shelter, and here again, brick was extensively used. In the houses at Woodchurch, he took great care in allocating both cupboard spaces and areas for prams and so on and appropriate exterior spaces and amenities – and the same applied in the flats in Birkenhead. The level of detail and concern for rational and clear planning, as well as civic duty, ran through all of his projects.

While post-war work was dominated by the Woodchurch housing estate, a large portion of Rowse's time was devoted to repairing the extensive bomb damage inflicted on India Buildings and George's Dock. India Buildings was particularly badly hit, and it required considerable effort to save the structure. It was decided to rebuild it as per the original specification, and some of the original artisans and craftsmen were re-employed.

Elsewhere, new opportunities were slowly opening up, and may have prompted Rowse's quick departure from the Woodchurch commission. In Belgium, he advised the government on post-war reconstruction and was awarded the Order of Leopold II in 1950 for his efforts.[1] The newly independent India had allocated a substantial area for a 'diplomatic colony' in New Delhi, and the Ministry of Works approached Rowse to design the British diplomatic enclave in 1951.[2] Rowse set out with his long-time collaborator Donald Bradshaw for India in April that year. As an admirer of Lutyens, Rowse would now, at last, get the chance to build within a city designed by him. Sadly, this was not to happen and Rowse ended up spending six weeks in hospital with typhoid. He returned to the UK in June, having achieved very little, and expenditure cuts in the UK caused further delay to the project. The Ministry of Works finally terminated the commission, deciding to undertake the work in-house, and Rowse's proposals for India remain unknown. Following 'irreconcilable differences', Bradshaw left the practice and Scarlett had already died towards the end of the war, leaving Rowse without his trusted collaborators.[3]

Rowse's interests had been somewhat diverted away from the practice as he began to spend increasing amounts of time at his properties in Anglesey (and served as Sheriff of Anglesey from 1942 to 1943), and following the illness he contracted in India, he sought respite in the West Indies during the winters.

Other more utilitarian projects, such as the Richmond sausage factory, offered some intrigue, but were of a different order to the works for which Rowse had become well known. There was a sense that the practice needed to be reformed, and Rowse's younger son (and by now collaborator) Christopher made a wise decision to invite Donald Bradshaw back to the practice, this time as partner, along with Thomas Harker. Shortly after, Rowse died at his home, Chapel House, Puddington, Cheshire on 22 March 1963 and was buried at St Nicholas' Church, Burton. Bradshaw designed his tombstone, a restrained and fitting monument based on a detail from Santa Maria Maggiore in Florence.

CONCLUSION

Gravestone of Herbert J Rowse in Burton, Cheshire

The practice was renamed Bradshaw, Rowse and Harker and, during the following years, the re-energised firm, with a fresh design outlook, started to win some major commissions for building types very familiar to the practice, including the new Mersey Tunnel extract tower at Seacombe, opened in 1971, and the extraordinary Midland Bank on Dale Street, of similar date. It did not resort to previous solutions, and sought new expressive, playful forms in glass, steel and exposed concrete, revealing a bold conviction that was perhaps also a reaction to the overshadowing designs produced by Rowse. While the formal resolution may have evolved and deliberately distanced itself from the practice's earlier work, the common threads of technological innovation, careful composition and an insistence on quality remained, however. It was these three elements, coupled with a desire to collaborate with artists, create lavish interiors and never overlook the civic duty of architecture, that had fundamentally steered Rowse's approach. And it was this final ambition, the civic duty, that really shines through in Rowse's home city of Liverpool, a city that is surely indebted to his architecture, sculpture and landscaping.

Notes

Introduction

1. Reilly, C 1933 *Architects' Journal* 77, 11 Jan 1933, 55.
2. Hyde, E 1993 'The life and work of Herbert James Rowse'. Unpublished MPhil thesis, Liverpool John Moores University, 8.

1 The early years

1. For more on this practice, *see* Carr, G 2014 'The Welsh builder in Liverpool' (lecture delivered at the Festival of Welsh Builders, 7 Jun 2014). http://www.liverpool-welsh.co.uk/archive/The%20Welsh%20Builders.pdf (accessed Feb 2019).
2. Budden, L (ed) 1932 *The Book of the Liverpool School of Architecture*. Liverpool: The University of Liverpool Press and London: Hodder and Stoughton, 34.
3. The history of the School has received considerable academic interest, *see* Powers, A 1982 'Architectural education in Britain'. Unpublished PhD thesis, University of Cambridge; Crinson, M and Lubbock, J 1994 *Architecture: Art of Profession? Three Hundred Years of Architectural Education in Britain*. Manchester: Manchester University Press; Sharples, J, Powers, A and Shippobottom, M 1996 *Charles Reilly and the Liverpool School of Architecture 1904–1933*. Liverpool: Liverpool University Press and an associated exhibition held at the Walker Art Gallery, Liverpool in 1996; Richmond, P 2001 *Marketing Modernisms: The Architecture and Influence of Charles Reilly*. Liverpool: Liverpool University Press; Crouch, C 2002 *Design Culture in Liverpool, 1880–1914: The Origins of the Liverpool School of Architecture*. Liverpool: Liverpool University Press; Dunne, J and Richmond, P 2008 *The World in One School: The History and Influence of the Liverpool School of Architecture 1894–2008*. Liverpool: Liverpool University Press.
4. Reilly, C 1906 *Portfolio of measured drawings / [by the students of the] School of Architecture, the University of Liverpool, 1906, Vol 1*. Liverpool: University Press of Liverpool; London: Crosby Lockwood, preface.
5. Reilly, C 1930 'Some younger architects of today: Herbert J Rowse'. *Building* v, Dec 1930, 524.
6. *See* University of Liverpool, Special Collections and Archives, 'Portfolio of measured drawings', School of Architecture, 1906–1908, SPEC 72.02.R36, Vol 2.
7. University of Liverpool, Special Collections and Archives, 'Measured work, School of Architecture, c 1909–1912', S3179.
8. Reilly 1930, 524.
9. *See* Richmond 2001 for further details.
10. Sharples, Powers and Shippobottom 1996, 7.
11. *See* Reilly, C (ed) 1911 *The Liverpool Architectural Sketch Book: Being the Annual of the School of Architecture of the University of Liverpool*, London: Architectural Review, Vol 2.
12. Frank Worthington Simon came to Liverpool from Edinburgh having won the competition for the Liverpool Cotton Exchange in 1905, as well as designing Orleans House in the city. *See* Simon's

obituary in *Journal of the Royal Institute of British Architects* **40**/15, 17 Jun 1933, 641.
13 Library and Archives Canada Ottawa, Ontario, Canada, 'Passenger Lists, 1865–1935'. Microfilm Reel No. T-4745.
14 The shipping records put Rowse in America for a shorter period of time than Reilly makes out in 'Some younger architects of today: Herbert J Rowse'. *Building* **v** Dec 1930, 524–9.
15 Reilly 1930, 526.
16 The US work-experience placements continued well into the early 1930s.
17 Records obtained from http://www.Ancestry.com UK, *Outward Passenger Lists, 1890–1960* [database on-line]. Provo, UT, USA: Ancestry.com Operations, 2012.
18 The folio was called *American Competitions*, (New York: Helburn and T-Square Club Philadelphia, 1913), and a copy remains in Rowse's former office at Martins Bank.
19 Herbert Rowse Obituary, RIBA Journal **70**, Oct 1963, 421–2.
20 These projects were all recorded in Budden 1932.
21 Rowse lived at Arrochar, Rocky Lane, Heswall.
22 Rowse's brother was Alfred George Rowse. He is listed as a concrete engineer on Principal Probate Registry. *Calendar of the Grants of Probate and Letters of Administration made in the Probate Registries of the High Court of Justice in England.*
23 There was also a Concrete House competition in 1933, sponsored by Cement Marketing Board.
24 Wirral Archives, Heswall Golf Club council minutes 1924–6, YHGC/M/C/1.
25 Lionnel Budden took over as Head of School when Reilly retired. He designed the war memorials at Liverpool and Birkenhead.

2 Monumental

1 Reilly, C 1910 (ed) *The Liverpool Architectural Sketch Book*. London: Architectural Review, vol 1, 'Introduction', 11–12.
2 Fry, E M 1975 *Autobiographical Sketches*. London: Elek Books, 47.
3 Reilly 1930, 526.
4 Falkus, M 1990 *The Blue Funnel Legend: History of the Ocean Steam Ship Company 1865–1973*. Basingstoke: Macmillan, 184.
5 See LPRO, India Buildings, 942.7213 IND.
6 The Bank of British West Africa was formed by Alfred Jones of Elder Dempster, a major rival and competitor of Holts, and the race for prestige buildings clearly resulted in this extraordinary collection of buildings being commissioned in the city.
7 Thornley was Chair of Liverpool Architectural Society at this time.
8 Reilly 1930, 528.
9 *Liverpolitan Magazine* **1**/1, May 1932, 16–17.
10 Reilly, quoted in *The Builder* **125**, 12 Oct 1923, 564.
11 *Liverpolitan Magazine* **1**/1, May 1932, 16–17.
12 Ibid.
13 See Cavanagh, T 1997 *Public Sculpture of Liverpool*. Liverpool: Liverpool University Press, 240.
14 Falkus 1990, 200.
15 Published as Corbett, H 1928 'The latest American building methods'. RIBA Journal **35**/7, 11 Feb 1928, 207–23.
16 See Hyde, E 1993 'The life and work of Herbert James Rowse'. Unpublished MPhil thesis, Liverpool John Moores University, 19.
17 See Booker, J 1990 *Temples of Mammon: The Architecture of Banking*. Edinburgh: Edinburgh University Press.
18 David, A J 1930 'Banks of Today'. *Building* **v**, Apr 1930, 155.

19 Of the London architects, Herbert Baker withdrew as he was too busy on the Bank of England project.
20 Barclays Group Archives (BGA), 'Bank of Liverpool and Martins Ltd. Minutes of Directors no. 15', minutes from 26 Mar 1926.
21 *See*, for example, the dog-legged corridor on the first–sixth floor plans, necessary because of the irregular shaped site.
22 Sharples, J 2006 *Liverpool*. New Haven, CT and London: Yale University Press, 168.
23 BGA, 'Bank of Liverpool and Martins Ltd. Minutes of Directors no. 15', minutes from 24 Aug 1926.
24 Various design developments were discussed, including the provision of the rooftop apartment for the manager and its associated colonnade, and the window frames were originally to be made from bronze.
25 *See* BGA, 'Bank of Liverpool and Martins Ltd. Minutes of Directors no. 15' and Building Committee minutes book, 0038-0571, 24 Aug 1926.
26 *See* Willis, C 1995 *Form Follows Finance: Skyscrapers and Skylines in New York and Chicago*. New York: Princeton Architectural Press, 65.
27 Rowse discussed this at length in his lecture to the Liverpool Architectural Society on 18 Jan 1933, transcript held at BGA, 0025–0162.
28 Reilly, C 1930 'New Headquarters, Martins Bank, Liverpool'. *Building* V, Apr 1930, 156.
29 Reilly, C 1932 'Martins Bank Liverpool'. *Building* 7, Nov 1932, 501.
30 Fraser, M and Kerr, J 2007 *Architecture and the 'Special Relationship': The American Influence on Post-War British Architecture*. London: Routledge, 72–3.
31 BGA, 'New head office building, Building Committee minutes book 1', minutes from 8 Mar 1927.
32 There were 20 columns, costed at £237 per column, around £10,000 each at 2018 prices.
33 Reilly 1930 *Building*.
34 Ibid.
35 Reilly, C 1926 'Architectural Notes: Bank Architecture'. *The Banker* 1, Jan 1926, 85–6.
36 Ibid, 89.
37 *See* Reilly, C 1924 *Masters of Architecture: McKim, Mead and White*. London: Ernest Benn. Rowse did not have a peninsula teller desk in his original proposal but provided a revised design 7 Jan 1927.
38 BGA, 'New head office building: Building committee minutes book 1', 8 Feb 1927.
39 When describing these features to the bank Building Committee, Rowse always stressed an American precedent as if to validate the decision. It seems that the Building Committee was also eager to have the latest in American innovation. BGA, 'New head office building: Building committee minutes book 1', 7 Jan 1927.
40 During World War II, the vaults were used by the Bank of England.
41 Both references were published in Falgàs, Victor de 1927 *Arte y decoración en España : arquitectura-arte decorativo* (Barcelona: Casellas Moncanut Hnos) and Rowse had a copy in his office.
42 For further details on the history of the bank, *see* Twomey, S 2014 'From monumental to modern: Martins Bank and Herbert J Rowse'. Unpublished MArch thesis, University of Liverpool.
43 *See* Poole, S J 1995 'A critical analysis of the work of Herbert Tyson Smith, sculptor and designer. Unpublished PhD thesis, University of Liverpool, 404.
44 Ibid.

45 Reilly, C *The Banker* **16**, Dec 1930, 382.
46 Reilly 1930, 528.
47 Lecture by Rowse to Liverpool Architectural Society, 18 Jan 1933, transcript held at BGA, 0025–0162.
48 Booker 1990, 247.
49 The ground floor of the bank has now been drastically altered and the elaborate carved doorway removed. *See* Cavanagh 1997, 22.
50 'Lloyds Bank, Church Street, Liverpool'. *Architects' Journal* **84**, 19 Oct 1932, 496–9.

3 Tunnel structures

1 Hyde, E 1993 'The life and work of Herbert James Rowse'. Unpublished MPhil thesis, Liverpool John Moores University, 7.
2 *See* 'A federation of Mersey Towns – important proposal to City Council – bid for improved cross-river transit'. *Liverpool Post and Mercury*, 2 Jan 1922, for useful background on the project.
3 The consultants' technical report is summarised in: 'Tunnel is the only way', *Liverpool Courier*, 27 Oct 1923, and *Liverpool Post and Mercury*, 27 Oct 1923. Original feasibility report in Liverpool Record Office, Minutes of Joint Tunnel Committee 1922-25, LIV 352 MIN/JOI 12/1.
4 The political manoeuvres of 1925 and subsequent arguments about tunnel entrances are the subject of continuing research. The events of 1925 (including disputes over tunnel technology) are reported at length in the minutes of evidence to the Parliamentary Select Committees that scrutinised the case for the private Mersey Tunnel Bill, 1925. Copies of the committee proceedings are in Liverpool Record Office (388/11/HOU) and are well covered in local newspapers from June (Lords) and July (Commons) 1925. The Act received royal assent in August as Ch. CX. [15&16 GEO.5.] Mersey Tunnel Act, 1925. Part II (7) provided that the minutes of the Liverpool and Birkenhead Joint Tunnel Committee should be deposited with the Town Clerks of Liverpool and Birkenhead. Only the 1922–5 volume (which preceded the Act) can be found. However, the Wirral Archive, Special Committee Minutes 1925–1948, B/060/5, contains, *inter alia*, the separate minutes kept by the Birkenhead (minority) group on the Joint Committee for part of the construction period. Our account leans heavily on contemporary newspaper reports and the official pamphlets published at intervals by the Joint Committee (which, in the absence of minutes, have to be treated with caution).
5 Liverpool Record Office, Short notes for Sir Thomas White and the Lord Mayor for Town Meeting, 21 Dec 1932, 352/JOI/10, and Liverpool Record Office, Manuscript Memoranda, 16 Dec 1932, HQ346. The Memoranda were written by Bertram Hewett, chief on-site engineer, for Sir Thomas White, who chaired the Mersey Tunnel Joint Committee following Sir Archibald Salvidge's death. The memoranda go into considerable detail on the reasons for the overspend. Sir Thomas was facing public meetings and an appearance before Parliamentary Select Committees in 1933 for the Bill authorising further borrowing.
6 The National Archives, 'Comparison of proposed vehicular tunnel and Hudson Road tunnel (New Jersey–New York, USA), Plans and Comparison', RAIL 475/235. Documents show the comparison of proposed vehicular tunnel and Hudson Road tunnel (New Jersey–New York, USA).

See also Jackson, R 2011 *Highway under the Hudson: A History of the Holland Tunnel*. New York: New York University Press, and Gillespie, A K 2011 *Crossing Under the Hudson: The Story of the Holland and Lincoln Tunnels*. Piscataway, NJ: Rutgers University Press.

7 Basil Mott, questioned in the Lords Select Committee by Moncrieff KC (representing opponents of the tunnel), Minutes of Evidence, 22 Jun 1925, 218, question 2173: 'Is there suction at the top? – No, there is no suction.'

8 'Thousands overcome by automobile exhaust'. *Pittsburgh Press*, 10 May 1924. See also 'Exhaust-and-supply ventilation of a long street tunnel'. *Engineering News Record* **94**, 1925, 764–7.

9 'Ventilating the tunnel: engineers report on experiments'. *Liverpool Post and Mercury*, 19 Feb 1931. The engineers' report, readers were told, would not be published.

10 'New Mersey Tunnel sensation: estimated deficit of £1,500,000'. *Liverpool Post and Mercury*, 18 Feb 1932; 'Catastrophe of new tunnel finances'. *Liverpool Evening Express*, 24 Feb 1932. An official pamphlet followed: White, T 1932 *Memorandum of the Chairman of the Mersey Tunnel Joint Committee on the Present Financial Position*. Liverpool: Liverpool Corporation. The pamphlet gives an expurgated account; for the real story see Hewett's memoranda (above, note 5).

11 Liverpool Record Office, Mersey Tunnel 1933 Bill Papers, containing 'Minutes of the Commons Select Committee', 14 Mar 1933, Hq346 at 4-47-B. Bertram Hewett explained to the committee, 'I would say that in 1925 the Engineer … could not foresee the magnitude and complexity of the ventilation problem.' (Answer to question 115).

12 *Liverpool Echo*, 20 Apr 1931.

13 *Liverpool Post and Mercury*, 8 May 1931.

14 *Liverpool Post and Mercury*, 25 Jul 1932 and 16 Sep 1932; *Architects' Journal* **76**, 28 Sep 1932.

15 The doors were also double skinned with a steel outer leaf, such was the concern over noise and vibration from the fans.

16 *Liverpool Post and Mercury*, 16 Sep 1932; *Architects' Journal* **76**, 28 Sep 1932.

17 *Liverpool Post and Mercury*, 3 Mar 1931. Hewett joined Mott's team in 1926 when the project was already underway, and evidently relied on office files and contacts for his 1932 briefing of Sir Thomas White and his evidence to Parliament in 1933. White had been appointed manager of the tunnel but died shortly before taking up the post.

18 Ibid.

19 *Liverpool Post and Mercury*, 17 Mar 1934.

20 *Liverpool Post and Mercury*, 18 Dec 1933.

21 *Liverpool Post and Mercury*, 2 Apr 1934.

22 Ibid.

23 Reports in *Liverpool Echo*, 11 Jun 1934, and *Liverpool Post and Mercury*, 21 and 29 Jun 1934.

24 Atkinson, E H W 1934 'Mersey Tunnel'. *The Architectural Review* **75**, Jun 1934, 202–4, and *Illustrated London News*, 14 Jul 1934.

25 *Radio Times*, 13 Jul 1934, provided extensive photographic coverage as well as advertising the live broadcasts of the opening and studio discussions. *The Times* supplement, 28 Apr 1934, came out before the opening with contributions from many of the tunnel's engineers, designers and product suppliers.

26 Towndrow, F 1934 'Through the Mersey Tunnel'. *The Observer*, 10 Jun 1934, 10.

4 Brick

1. Reilly, C 1938 'The Glasgow Exhibition: second thoughts'. *Manchester Guardian*, 22 Jun 1938, 11.
2. Cotton, V E and Mountford, J F 1951 *The Story of Liverpool: An Exhibition Devised and Presented by the Liverpool Corporation and Liverpool University for the Festival Year 1951*. Liverpool: Tinling and Co, 55. For a detailed overview of the Philharmonic's history, *see* Henley, D and McNulty, M 2009 *The Original Liverpool Sound: The Royal Liverpool Philharmonic Story*. Liverpool: Liverpool University Press.
3. *The Liverpolitan* **8**/6, Jun 1939, 20–1.
4. Ibid.
5. Ibid.
6. *See* Liverpool Public Records Office (LPRO), Philharmonic Hall Archive (PHA), 'Ninety-sixth report of the committee', 23 May 1935, 780PHI/1/2/85–91. They rehearsed and performed at the Central Methodist Hall on Renshaw Street and St George's Hall.
7. Sir Henry Wood quoted in, LPRO/PHA, 'Ninety-sixth report of the committee', 23 May 1935, 780PHI/1/2/85-91
8. Ibid.
9. *The Liverpolitan* **5**/6, Jun 1936, 16–17.
10. Ibid.
11. LPRO/PHA, 'Philharmonic Specification and Bill of Quantities', Apr 1937, 1.
12. LPRO/PHA, 'Letter to the Proprietors', 12 May 1936, 780PHI/1/2/85–91.
13. LPRO/PHA, 'Meeting of Building Committee', 23 Feb 1937, 780PHI/9/2/1.
14. LPRO/PHA, 'Ninety-ninth report of the Committee', Apr 1938, 780PHI/9/2/1.
15. *See* LPRO/PHA, H J Rowse, New Philharmonic Hall leaflet, 1939, 780 PHI/1/8/3.
16. Dunne, J and Richmond, P 2008 *The World in One School: The History and Influence of the Liverpool School of Architecture 1894–2008*. Liverpool: Liverpool University Press, 24, 26.
17. *See* University of Liverpool, Special Collections and Archives, 'Fifth year thesis design for a Civic Concert Hall for Liverpool by A E Rice', S3204/7B/19.
18. LPRO/PHA, P H Naftel to Chairman of Philharmonic Society, 10 Jun 1936, 780PHI/9/2/1.
19. *See* LPRO/PHA, H J Rowse, New Philharmonic Hall leaflet, 1939, 780 PHI/1/8/3.
20. Reputed to be the last surviving example in the world.
21. *The Liverpolitan* **5**/6, Jun 1936, 16–17.
22. Ibid.
23. Whistler was on the staff at Pilkington's in-house architecture and design studio.
24. Hodel also did a commemorative bowl for the opening of the Mersey Tunnels, now held in the Liverpool Town Hall.
25. McGrath, R 1937 *Glass in Architecture and Decoration*. London: Architectural Press.
26. *See* Holder, J 1994 'Reflecting change: Pilkington as a patron of modern architecture and design' in Stamp, G, Lever, J and Powers, A (eds) 1994 *Industrial Architecture* (*Twentieth Century Architecture* special issue **1**). London: Twentieth Century Society, Oct 1994, 65–76.
27. Pinkham, R 1982 'Interview with Sigmund Pollitzer'. *Thirties Society Journal* **2**, 5–12.
28. Holder 1994, 71.
29. Pilkington Brothers' glass works offices, Kirk Sandall, near Doncaster; Architects: T H Johnson & Son. *Architect & Building News*, 13 Nov 1936, 201.
30. *See* Smiles, S (ed) 1998 *Going Modern and Being British: Art, Architecture and Design in Devon 1910–1960*. Exeter: Intellect, 148.
31. Holder 1994, 71.

32 McGrath, R 1939 'Glass in construction and decoration'. *Architectural Review* **85**, Feb 1939, 100–8.
33 Pilkington Brothers Limited nd *Vitrolite Specifications*. St Helens: Pilkington Brothers Limited; MacGrath, R 1937 *Glass in Architecture and Decoration*. London: Architectural Press.
34 Barker 1977, 344.
35 Ibid, 372.
36 Ibid, 371. See also Holder 1994, 71.
37 Pilkington Archive, Head Office Grove Street, Notes from rear of Neg 4458–1, 1/1/7/33.
38 Yeomans, D 1998 'The pre-history of the curtain wall'. *Construction History* **14**, 59–82, and Holder, 1994, 70.
39 Cheesman and Pollitzer both advised Oliver Hill on this project. See also RIBA, Oliver Hill Papers, 'Boudoir with walls, floor and furniture entirely of glass. Designed by Oliver Hill' (typescript issued to the architectural press, undated), HiO/79/1.
40 Pilkington Archive, Sheet Works Showroom, Notes from rear of Neg 105/18/7, 1/1/7/54.
41 Pollitzer also designed some of the interior fit-out on RMS *Queen Mary*. See https://cinemafan2.livejournal.com/12842.html (accessed February 2019).
42 Pinkham, R 1982 'Interview with Sigmund Pollitzer'. *Thirties Society Journal* **2**, 5–12, 6.
43 Pilkington would later revolutionise plate float glass production. They commissioned a new headquarters in 1959 complete with glazed façades and extensive use of their products designed by Maxwell Fry and Jane Drew, *see* Holland, J and Jackson, I 2013 'A monument to humanism: Pilkington Brothers' headquarters (1955–1965) by Fry, Drew and Partners'. *Architectural History* **56**, 343–86.
44 *See* Yeomans 1998.
45 Edward Carter Preston designed much of the statuary at the Liverpool Anglican Cathedral as well as creating the designs for several medals. He was also Tyson Smith's brother-in-law. *See also* Compton, A (ed) 1999 *Edward Carter Preston, 1885–1965: Sculptor, Painter, Medallist*. Liverpool: University of Liverpool Art Collections.
46 Reilly 1938, 11.
47 Cheeseman, K 1941 'Designing glass for architectural and interior design uses'. *Art and Industry*, Oct 1941, 110–116, 112–113.
48 *See The Builder* **172**, 25 Apr 1947, 395–8 and *Architects' Journal* **107**, 11 Mar 1948, 237–9.
49 The School received its Royal Charter as the University of London's School of Pharmacy in 1952 (*The Times*, 17 Jun 1952, 9). The Society moved from its original home at No. 17 Bloomsbury Square into a series of temporary buildings before occupying its present Dockland headquarters.
50 *Pharmaceutical Journal* **160**, 29 May 1937.
51 University College of London (UCL), School of Pharmacy, Pharmaceutical Society, Secretary's Report, 5 Mar 1934.
52 UCL, Minutes of Sub-Committee on Premises, A R Melhuish, Chairman, 5 Mar 1934.
53 Hudson, B 2013 *The School of Pharmacy, University of London: Medicines, Science and Society, 1842–2012*, London: Academic Press, 111.
54 UCL, Pharmaceutical Society, Cost Report 1936.
55 UCL, Pharmaceutical Society, Report on the Finances of the New Building by F G Adams, 29 Oct 1936.
56 Hudson 2013, 122.
57 UCL, Building costs, Memo by Treasurer, 1 Sep 1937.

58 UCL, The Society's New Headquarters, Secretary's Report, 30 Aug 1938, signed by H N Linstead, 4.
59 UCL, Minutes of a Special Meeting of the Finance Committee, 5 Sep 1938.
60 *Pharmaceutical Journal* **161**, 3 Dec 1938, 584, and 10 Dec 1938, 611.
61 Ibid, 24 Dec 1938, 656.
62 Ibid, 15 Oct 1938, 400.
63 *Pharmaceutical Journal* **162**, 15 Aug 1939, 390.
64 Ibid, 29 Apr 1939, 446.
65 Ibid, 23 Sep 1939, 318, and 14 Oct 1939, 368.
66 *Pharmaceutical Journal* **164**, 27 Jan 1940, 58.
67 A photograph in *The Builder* **172**/5436, 25 Apr 1947, 395, shows the state that building work had reached by 1940: some of the excavated spoil was still in front of the building but cranes had been removed.

5 Social housing and planning

1 'The Prestatyn Estate, North Wales: competition for layout'. *The Builder* **102**/3609, 5 Apr 1912, 399.
2 *Building*, Dec 1930, 525–6.
3 The 1930 Act subsidised the number of people rehoused, not the number of dwellings. This principle was retained for subsequent campaigns designed to reduce overcrowding.
4 Newbery, F 1980 'Liverpool's flats: policy and design of Central Area Redevelopment by the Liverpool Housing Department'. Unpublished BArch dissertation, University of Liverpool School of Architecture, 1980. *See also* Whitfield, M 2010 'Multi-storey public housing in Liverpool during the inter-war years'. Unpublished PhD thesis, Manchester Metropolitan University.
5 Newbery 1980, 103.
6 Wirral Archives, Birkenhead Estates Committee, Minutes, 9 Oct 1931, B/033/3, 136.
7 Ibid, Minutes, 12 Feb 1932, 179.
8 Ibid, Minutes, 11 Mar 1932, 192.
9 Ibid, Minutes, 7 Oct 1932, 266. For subsequent progress: Minutes, 9 Dec 1932, 291–2; 13 Jan 1933, 303–4; 10 Mar 1933, 330.
10 *Birkenhead News*, 4 Feb 1933, 5.
11 *Birkenhead News*, 6 May 1933, 3.
12 For the 10-storey cylindrical blocks, *see* 'Planning for standardisation: a scheme for ten-storey circular flats'. *Architects' Journal* **80**, 25 Oct 1934, 587, 600-1 and 1 Nov 1934, 623–4 plus Green, D 'Circular Building', Ibid, 651–2. Green was Managing Director of Truscon, the company that had developed the system in collaboration with Launcelot Keay's city architecture department.
13 Wirral Archives, Minutes of the Special Meeting of Estates Committee, 3 Apr 1935, B/033/3, 75.
14 Wirral Archives, Minutes of Special Meeting 17 Jun 1935, B/033/3, 107.
15 The agricultural land was purchased from Sir Ernest Royden in 1926 for £69,000.
16 Hubbard, E and Shippobottom, M 1988 *Guide to Port Sunlight Village*. Liverpool: Liverpool University Press, 21.
17 *Birkenhead News*, 16 Sept 1933, 2.
18 *Birkenhead News*, 9 Dec 1933, 3.
19 *Birkenhead News*, 4 Nov 1933, 6.
20 *Birkenhead News*, 7 Oct 1933, 3 and 7; 28 Oct, 3; 9 Dec, 3.
21 *Birkenhead News*, 9 Dec 1933, 3.
22 Ibid.
23 Wirral Archives, Birkenhead Borough Council (BBC), Housing Committee Minutes (HCM), 28 Jul 1943, B/033/3, 442–3, minute 132: Councillor Lloyd,

seconded by Alderman Prentice, proposed that the appointee be a member both of the RIBA and TPI with responsibility for land negotiations and purchase, advice on town planning and design of new buildings, unless otherwise dictated by Council.

24 Wirral Archives, BBC, HCM, 3 Nov 1943, B/042/3, 505–7, minute 176. Birkenhead's first Borough Architect, with his own department and responsibility for both building and planning, was authorised in 1948 (BBC, HCM, 10 Dec 1948, B/042/3, 464–5, minute 551). It was then delayed by Finance Committee's suggestion that the post be combined with Director of Housing (BBC, HCM, 14 Jan 1949, B/042/3, 482, minute 603).

25 University of Liverpool, Special Collections and Archives, Terms of Appointment, D207/3/9. The contract was dated 26 Feb 1944: 1,000 guineas fee, first-class travel for Reilly, third-class for his colleagues; 20s daily hotel and living expenses. The Plan was supposed to take a year.

26 *See* University of Liverpool, Special Collections and Archives, 'Press cuttings relating to Reilly's views on post-war reconstruction and his involvement with the Town and Country Planning Association (TCPA), 28 October 1943 – 26 February 1944', D207/17/2.

27 On Reilly's new interest in social planning, late in his time at Liverpool, *see* Holford's obituary tribute, 'Sir Charles Reilly'. *Architectural Review*, May 1948, 181–3. For his interest in Soviet planning, *see* Potter, L 1998 'National tensions in the post war planning of local authority housing and the "Woodchurch controversy"'. Unpublished PhD thesis, University of Liverpool.

28 The Council explained, 'Professor Reilly was engaged by Birkenhead to make a general planning scheme for the town. Such a scheme involved such things as the location of heavy industry, commercial and residential districts, main roads, shopping centres, civic centre, general appearance of the town, river front, etc. The layout of a particular housing estate was not a part of his functions and Professor Reilly was never requested by the Estates Committee to do this.' *Birkenhead News*, 8 Jun 1944.

29 *See* the handwritten notes on Reilly's plan, Wirral Archives, B/804/9e.

30 There was concern from some factions of the Conservative council that 'Russian' films might be screened.

31 *The Tribune*, 16 Jun 1944, 11.

32 8 July 1944, and reprinted as 'Birkenhead: community versus segregation'. *Architects' Journal* **100**, 3 Aug 1944, 85–7.

33 Wolfe, L 1945 *The Reilly Plan: A New Way of Life*. London: Nicholson & Watson.

34 L Potter's PhD thesis provides an excellent critique of the Reilly plan and some of its fundamental problems.

35 Wirral Archive, Birkenhead Town Clerk's files, letter to RIBA 21 Jul 1944, reply from RIBA 27 Jul 1944, B/110/218–221.

36 'Liverpool Architect to design houses'. *Birkenhead News*, 9 Sep 1944.

37 'Conservatives adopt Rowse plan'. *Birkenhead News*, 10 Mar 1945.

38 From where had Reilly gleaned his ideas about the narrow-fronted house? For pre-war thinking on high-density low-rise housing, *see* Edwards, A T 1946 *Modern Terrace Houses: Researches on High-Density Development*. London: Tiranti, for the Chadwick Trust. Elizabeth Denby proposed 'A novel housing scheme at the "Ideal

Home" Exhibition'. *Architect & Building News*, 14 Apr 1939, 25–7. On Denby *see* Darling, E 'The house that is a woman's book come true: the all-Europe house and four women's spatial practices in inter-war England' in Darling, E and Whitworth, L (eds) 2007 *Women and the Making of Built Space in England 1870–1950*. Aldershot: Ashgate, 123–40.
39 Potter, L 1998 'National tensions in the post war planning of local authority housing and the "Woodchurch controversy"'. Unpublished PhD thesis, University of Liverpool, 110.
40 'The Rowse plan for Woodchurch'. *Birkenhead News*, 13 Jan 1945.
41 *Architect & Building News*, 13 Oct 1950, 406.
42 Reilly, C and Aslan, N J 1947 *Outline Plan for the County Borough of Birkenhead*. Birkenhead: Birkenhead Borough Council, 93–4.
43 Stephenson, G 1950 'MOH housing medal awards'. *Architects' Journal* **112**/2912, 21 Dec 1950, 549.
44 Potter 1998, 124–5.
45 Ibid.
46 *See* Wirral Archives, b/804/39.
47 Owens, R 1987 'Born Again'. *Architects' Journal* **185**, 18 Mar 1987, 44–57.

6 Conclusion

1 Pepper, S and Richmond, P *Oxford Dictionary of National Biography*. https://doi.org/10.1093/ref:odnb/40913 (accessed Feb 2019).
2 See Bertram, M 2017 *Room for Diplomacy: The History of Britain's Diplomatic Buildings Overseas 1800–2000*. Salisbury: Spire Books, 280.
3 Hyde, E 1993 'The life and work of Herbert James Rowse'. Unpublished MPhil thesis, Liverpool John Moores University.

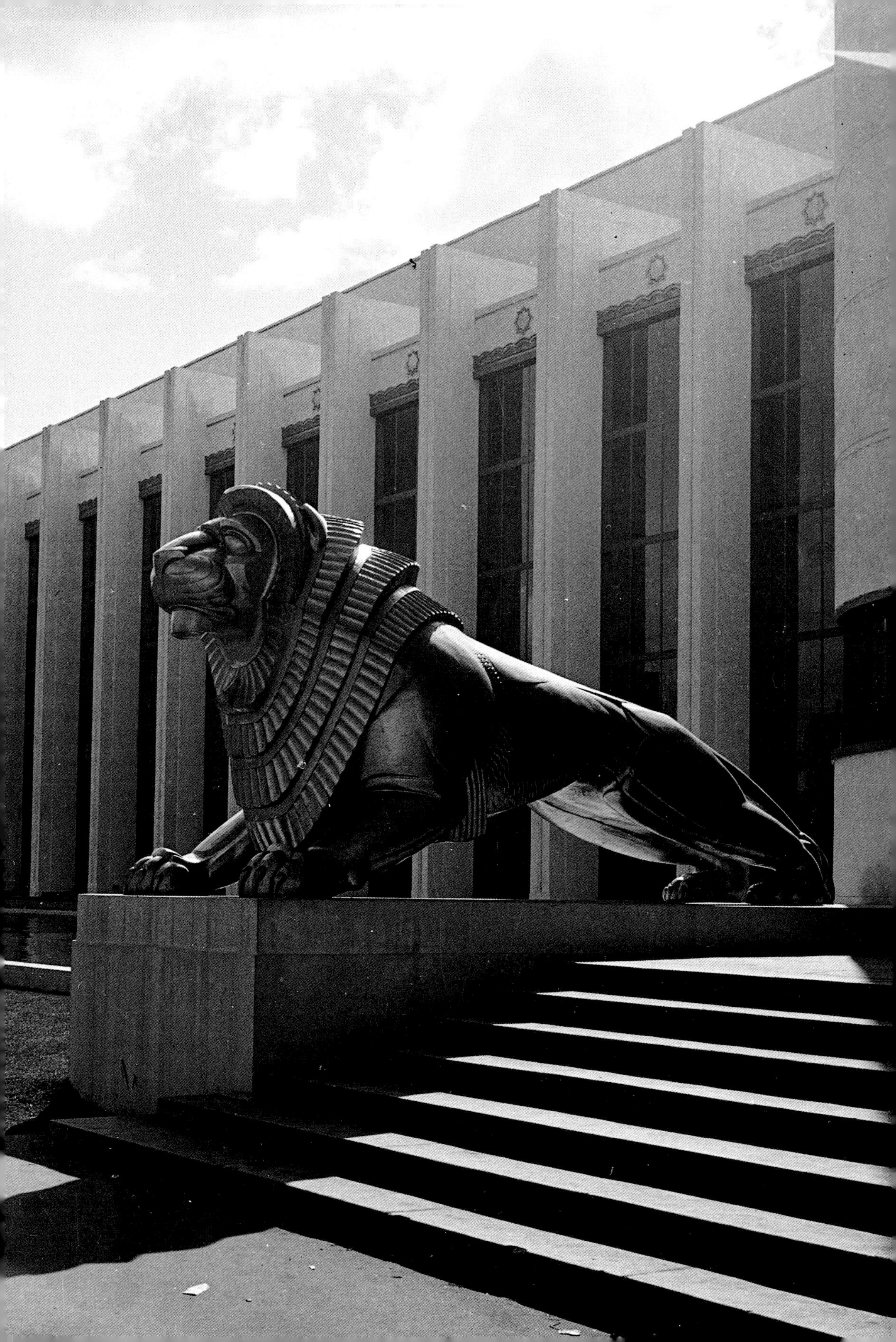

List of works

*   Substantially altered or partly demolished
**   Demolished
*** Unbuilt
Bold type indicates works profiled in this book

1911
Coventry Town Hall***
Competition organised by Coventry City Council; Rowse's design was placed third
The Builder **100**/3560, 28 Apr 1911, 524–8

1912
Housing at Prestatyn, North Wales***
Competition organised by the Prestatyn Estate (commended)
Designed with Sydney A Kelly
The Builder **102**/3609, 5 Apr 1912, 397–9

1918
Glencaple
Blundellsands, Crosby, Lancashire
Conservatory, internal remodelling of house and garden layout
Client: Sir Robert Lowdon Connell
Architectural Review **51**, Jan–Jun 1922, 168–9
Budden, L (ed) 1932 *The Book of the Liverpool School of Architecture*. Liverpool: The University of Liverpool Press and London: Hodder and Stoughton, plate CXX

1918
Sugar refinery, Liverpool
Client: Messrs Manbré and Garton (Liverpool Saccharine Co)
Budden, L (ed) 1932 *The Book of the Liverpool School of Architecture*. Liverpool: The University of Liverpool Press and London: Hodder and Stoughton, plate CXLV

1919–24
Hulton Avenue housing estate
Cumber Lane, Whiston, Rainhill, Lancashire
Client: Whiston Rural District Council (at the instigation of Lord Aberconway)
Building **5**/12, Dec 1930, 524–9

1921
Allandale (house)
Farr Hall Road, Heswall, Cheshire
Client: Mr Parry (Rowse's wife's uncle)

One of the two golden lions flanking the entrance steps of the United Kingdom Pavilion, Empire Exhibition, Glasgow

1921
Millmead (house)
Mill Lane, Willaston, Cheshire
Client: Sarah Ann Rowse (Rowse's mother)
Architectural Review **51**, Jan–Jun 1922, 173
Budden, L (ed) 1932 The Book of the Liverpool School of Architecture. Liverpool: The University of Liverpool Press and London: Hodder and Stoughton, plate CIX
Good Housekeeping, Mar 1992, 99–100

1923
House at Thurstaston, Cheshire

1923
Library and chambers, King's College, Cambridge***
Designed with Lionel B Budden
Architects' Journal **58**/1505, 7 Nov 1923, 683–8; /1506, 14 Nov 1923, 728–9; /1507, 21 Nov 1923, 775–6
The Builder **126**/4240, 9 May 1924, 754
Building **5**/12, Dec 1930, 524–9
Buildings for the Fellows of King's College, Cambridge. The bursar was J Maynard Keynes, who organised an invited competition for architects under 45, assessed by C Lovett Gill. Rowse and Budden were declared the winners, but the decision was disputed and the scheme abandoned.

1923–32
India Buildings
Water Street, Liverpool
Client: Alfred Holt & Co (office buildings for Blue Funnel Line)
Designed with Arnold Thornley
Listed at grade II in 1975 and grade II* in 2003

Budden, L B 1923 'The Liverpool Shipping Office Competition'. Architects' Journal **58**/1500, 3 Oct 1923, 491–4
Architect & Building News **115**/2991, 16 Apr 1926, 348–9
Architect & Building News **116**/3003, 9 Jul 1926, 47–50
Architects' Journal **73**, 14 Jan 1931, 44–7
Ellis, S H 1932 'India Buildings'. Liverpool Engineering Society Transactions **54**, 1932–3, 85–120
Hyde, F E and Harris, J R 1956 Blue Funnel: A History of Alfred J. Holt & Company of Liverpool from 1865 to 1914. Liverpool: Liverpool University Press, 8
Poole, S J 1995 'A critical analysis of the work of Herbert Tyson Smith, sculptor and designer'. Unpublished PhD thesis, University of Liverpool, 444
Cavanagh, T 1997 Public Sculpture of Liverpool. Liverpool: Liverpool University Press, 240
War damaged in 1941 and reconstructed under Rowse's supervision from 1945

1924
Garthlands
Gayton Lane, Heswall, Cheshire
Architects' Journal **71**, 4 Jun 1930, 857–8

1924
York Cottage
55 St Helen's Road, Ormskirk, Lancashire
Building **5**/12, Dec 1930, 524–9
Budden, L (ed) 1932 The Book of the Liverpool School of Architecture. Liverpool: The University of Liverpool Press and London: Hodder and Stoughton, plate CVII

York Cottage, St Helen's Road, Ormskirk

1925
Heswall Golf Club
Cottage Lane, Gayton, Cheshire
Building **5**/12, Dec 1930, 524–9
Hyde, E 1993 'The life and work of Herbert James Rowse'. Unpublished MPhil thesis, Liverpool John Moores University, 60–9

1925
House, Menlove Gardens, Liverpool

1925–34
Queensway Mersey Tunnel
Liverpool & Birkenhead
Client: Mersey Joint Committee (Liverpool and Birkenhead councils)
Engineers: Basil Mott and John Alexander Brodie
Listed at grade II in 1980
Mersey Tunnel Joint Committee 1934 *The Story of the Mersey Tunnel Officially Named Queensway*. *Queensway Mersey Tunnel Souvenir Album*, Stewart Bale Collection, Merseyside Maritime Museum Archives & Library, 1934
Liverpool: Charles Birchall (Liverpool Central Library Archives)
Atkinson, E H W 1934 'Mersey Tunnel'. *Architectural Review* **75**, Jun 1934, 229
Liverpool Daily Post, supplement, 16 Jul 1934, 23
Anderson, D 'The Construction of the Mersey Tunnel'. *Journal of the Institution of Civil Engineers* **2**/6, 1936, 473–544
Wonders of World Engineering, no. 2, 9 Mar 1937, 39–44
Moore, J 1988 *Underground Liverpool*. Liverpool: Bluecoat Press
Poole, S J 1995 'A critical analysis of the work of Herbert Tyson Smith, sculptor and designer'. Unpublished PhD thesis, University of Liverpool, 444
Formally opened by King George V on 18 Jul 1934. Rowse was responsible for the tunnel entrances at Old Haymarket and at New Quay, along with a number of associated ventilation stations. He was also responsible for the tunnel interior – now altered – which had a black glass dado framed with stainless steel.

1927
Lloyds Bank
Woolton Road/Heathfield Road,
Liverpool
Hyde, E 1993 'The life and work of Herbert J Rowse'. Unpublished MPhil thesis, Liverpool John Moores University, 125, 130

1927
West Hey house
Dawstone Road, Heswall, Cheshire
Remodelling of an existing Victorian house

1927–32
Martins Bank headquarters
Water Street, Liverpool
Listed at grade II* in 1966
The Builder **130**/4339, 2 Apr 1926, 551, 553–5
Architects' Journal **63**/1631, 7 Apr 1926, 525–31
Building **5**/4, Apr 1930, 156–76
The Builder **143**/4682, 28 Oct 1932, 718, 722–8
Architects' Journal **76**, 2 Nov 1932, 549–53 and supplement
Budden, L (ed) 1932 *The Book of the Liverpool School of Architecture*. Liverpool: The University of Liverpool Press and London: Hodder and Stoughton, plates CXXXIV–V
Architects' Journal **77**, 11 Jan 1933, 55
The Liverpolitan **3**/9, Sep 1934, 10; **5**/8, Aug 1936, 14; **5**/9, Sep 1936, 22
Chandler, G 1964 *Four Centuries of Banking* 1. London: Batsford, 487
Hughes, Q 1999 *Liverpool: City of Architecture*. Liverpool: Bluecoat Press, 144–5
Hyde, E 1993 'The life and work of Herbert J Rowse'. Unpublished MPhil thesis, Liverpool John Moores University, Appendix: Reminiscences of Rex Brown, 20–2
Poole, S J 1995 'A critical analysis of the work

Midas medallion, Martins Bank

of Herbert Tyson Smith, sculptor and designer'. Unpublished PhD thesis, University of Liverpool, 444

Sharples, J 2004 *Liverpool* (Pevsner Architectural Guides). Newhaven, CT and London: Yale University Press, 168–70

Twomey, S 2014 'From monumental to modern: Martins Bank and Herbert J Rowse'. Unpublished MArch dissertation, University of Liverpool Offices and banking premises for Martins Bank. Won in an invited competition assessed in 1926 by C H Reilly.

1929
Interior designs for Compania Sud Americana

1929
Levanton
Charcoal Road, Bowden, Cheshire

1930
J Bibby & Sons Ltd
Great Howard Street, Liverpool
Hyde, E 1993 'The life and work of Herbert J Rowse'. Unpublished MPhil thesis, Liverpool John Moores University, 137–8

1930
Headquarters building
Barcelona, Spain
Client: Compania Aplicacionas Electricas SA
Hyde, E 1993 'The life and work of Herbert J Rowse'. Unpublished MPhil thesis, Liverpool John Moores University, 142–3

1930
Fire Salvage Association of Liverpool

Headquarters building, Compania Aplicacionas Electricas SA, Barcelona, Spain

1930
Portable bank for Martins Bank
Building 5/12, Dec 1930, 524–9
Budden, L (ed) 1932 *The Book of the Liverpool School of Architecture*. Liverpool: The University of Liverpool Press and London: Hodder and Stoughton, plate CXLIII

c 1930
Lloyds Bank
Childwall, Lancashire
Budden, L (ed) 1932 *The Book of the Liverpool School of Architecture*. Liverpool: The University of Liverpool Press and London: Hodder and Stoughton, plate CXLII

1930–1
Lloyds Bank★
17 Church Street, Liverpool
Building **5**/12, Dec 1930, 524–9
Building **7**/1, Jan 1932, 25–6
Architects' Journal **76**, 19 Oct 1932, 496–9; 23 Nov 1932, 677
Architecture Illustrated **6**/5, May 1933, 138–9
Cavanagh, T 1997 *Public Sculpture of Liverpool*. Liverpool: Liverpool University Press, 22
Poole, S J 1995 'A critical analysis of the work of Herbert Tyson Smith, sculptor and designer'. Unpublished PhD thesis, University of Liverpool, 444
Carved decorations in Portland stone are by Herbert Tyson Smith and Edmund C Thompson.
The building is now a shop and the carved main entrance surround has been demolished.

1931
St Paul's Eye Hospital
Old Hall Street, Liverpool
Building **5**/12, Dec 1930, 524–9
Hyde, E 1993 'The life and work of Herbert J Rowse'. Unpublished MPhil thesis, Liverpool John Moores University, 138–40

1931–4
George's Dock Ventilation and Control Station★
Pier Head, Liverpool
Client: Mersey Joint Committee (Liverpool and Birkenhead councils)
Listed at grade II in 1980
Architects' Journal **76**, 28 Sep 1932, 393–4
'The Mersey Tunnel', *Building* **9**/5, May 1934, 172–5

Daily Post & Mercury, 16 May 1934, 13
Atkinson, E H W 1934 'Mersey Tunnel'. *Architectural Review* **75**, Jun 1934, 229
Liverpool Daily Post, 18 Apr 1935, 6
Stamp, G 1989 'Architectural Sculpture in Liverpool', in P Curtis (ed) *Patronage and Practice: Sculpture on Merseyside*. Liverpool: Tate Gallery, 8–12
Cavanagh, T 1997 *Public Sculpture of Liverpool*. Liverpool: Liverpool University Press, 22
Following war damage, the building was reconstructed by Rowse in 1951–2
Hughes, Q 1999 *Liverpool: City of Architecture*. Liverpool: Bluecoat Press, 151

1931–4
New Quay Ventilation Station
Fazakerley Street, Liverpool
Client: Mersey Joint Committee (Liverpool and Birkenhead councils)
Listed at grade II in 1980
Architects' Journal **79**, 3 May 1934, 634–6
Sharples, J 2004 *Liverpool* (Pevsner Architectural Guides). Newhaven, CT and London: Yale University Press, 160

1931–4
North John Street Ventilation Station
North John Street, Liverpool
Client: Mersey Joint Committee (Liverpool and Birkenhead councils)
Listed at grade II in 1980
Sculptures: Edmund C Thompson
Architects' Journal **76**, 28 Dec 1932, 813
Architects' Journal **79**, 3 May 1934, 634–6
Daily Post, 18 Apr 1935, 6
Sharples, J 2004 *Liverpool* (Pevsner Architectural Guides). Newhaven, CT and London: Yale University Press, 156

LIST OF WORKS

1931–4
Old Haymarket Tunnel Entrance*
Old Haymarket, Liverpool
Client: Mersey Joint Committee
(Liverpool and Birkenhead councils)
Listed at grade II in 1980
The Liverpolitan **3**/8, Aug 1934, 20
Hughes, Q 1999 *Liverpool: City of Architecture*. Liverpool: Bluecoat Press, 143
Sharples, J 2004 *Liverpool* (Pevsner Architectural Guides). Newhaven, CT and London: Yale University Press, 161–2
The statues of King George V and Queen Mary were moved in the early 1970s to accommodate the construction of the Churchill flyover. The layout in front of the tunnel has also had changes made to Rowse's original conception, the most significant being the loss of the large lighting column, faced with black granite, that once stood directly opposite the tunnel entrance.

1931–4
Sidney Street Ventilation Station
Birkenhead
Client: Mersey Joint Committee
(Liverpool and Birkenhead councils)
Listed at grade II in 1980
Architects' Journal **76**, 28 Dec 1932, 814
Atkinson, E H W 'Mersey Tunnel'. *Architectural Review* **75**, Jun 1934, 229
The Story of the Mersey Tunnel Officially Named Queensway, Liverpool, Charles Birchall & Sons for the Mersey Tunnel Joint Committee, 1934 (Liverpool Central Library Archives)

1931–4
Taylor Street Ventilation Station
Birkenhead
Client: Mersey Joint Committee
(Liverpool and Birkenhead councils)
Listed at grade II in 1980
Architects' Journal **76**, 28 Dec 1932, 813

1931–4
Woodside Ventilation Station
Birkenhead
Client: Mersey Joint Committee
(Liverpool and Birkenhead councils)
RIBA Bronze Medal, 1937
Listed at grade II in 1980
The Builder **153**/4942, 22 Oct 1937, 720

1933–9
Philharmonic Hall
Hope Street, Liverpool
Listed at grade II* in 1981
Liverpool Daily Post Supplement, 16 Jul 1934, 23
The Liverpolitan **3**/9, Sep 1934, 5; **4**/9, Sep 1935, 11; **5**/6, Jun 1936, 16–17; **6**/11, Nov 1937, 20; **7**/5, May 1938, 7; **8**/6, Jun 1939, 21; **22**/7, Jul 1953, 28; **22**/8, Aug 1953, 3
Architects' Journal **83**, 4 Jun 1936, 862
The Builder **151**/4874, 3 Jul 1936, 9–11
The Builder **157**/5031, 7 Jul 1939, 11–16
Architects' Journal **90**, 24 Aug 1939, 273–5
Architectural Review **86**, Oct 1939, 155–6;
Hyde, E 1989 'The shape of a megaphone'. *Architects' Journal* **190**/6, 9 Aug, 77
Cavanagh, T 1997 *Public Sculpture of Liverpool*. Liverpool: Liverpool University Press, 80–1
Hyde, E 1993 'The life and work of Herbert J Rowse'. Unpublished MPhil thesis, Liverpool John Moores University, Appendix: Reminiscences of Rex Brown, 15–18
Hughes, Q 1999 *Liverpool: City of Architecture*. Liverpool: Bluecoat Press, 149
Sharples, J 2004 *Liverpool* (Pevsner Architectural Guides). Newhaven, CT and London: Yale University Press, 31, 33, 234–6
Henley, D and McKernan, V 2009 *The Original Liverpool Sound*. Liverpool: Liverpool University Press, 107–10

1934
Council flats for Birkenhead Council (later known as St Andrews Square)
Client: Birkenhead Municipality
Camden Street, Birkenhead, Cheshire

1934
Alterations at Rocklands
House at Thornton Hough, Cheshire
Hyde, E 1993 'The life and work of Herbert J Rowse'. Unpublished MPhil thesis, Liverpool John Moores University, 142

1935–60
Headquarters for the Pharmaceutical Society of Great Britain
Completed and opened as the University of London Pharmacy School and Examination Laboratories (1960), now the School of Pharmacy, University College London (since 2012).
University College London, Brunswick Square
Architects' Journal **107**/2770, 11 Mar 1948, 237
The Builder **153**/4942, 22 Oct 1937, 722
The Builder **172**/5436, 25 Apr 1947, 395–8
Hyde, E 1993 'The life and work of Herbert J Rowse'. Unpublished MPhil thesis, Liverpool John Moores University, Appendix: Reminiscences of Rex Brown, 15
Wallis, T E 1964 *History of the School of Pharmacy*. London: Pharmaceutical Press, 80–1

1935
Alterations to Puddington Hall and two cottages
Client: Mr W W Higgins
Hyde, E 1993 'The life and work of Herbert J Rowse'. Unpublished MPhil thesis, Liverpool John Moores University, 136, 142

1936
New premises for Littlewood's Mail Order*
Aintree, Lancashire
Work suspended by outbreak of World War II and later abandoned
Hyde, E 1993 'The life and work of Herbert J Rowse'. Unpublished MPhil thesis, Liverpool John Moores University, 172

1936
Offices and canteen for Pilkington Bros*
Grove Street, St Helens, Lancashire
Client: Pilkington Bros
Listed at grade II in 1985
Architectural Review **89**, May 1941, 97–8
Architects' Journal **94**, 17 Jul 1941, 47–8
Building Design, no. 1056, 8 Nov 1991, 4
Holder, J 1994 'Reflecting change: Pilkington as a patron of modern architecture and design'. *Twentieth Century Society Journal* **1**: Industrial Architecture, 73–6
Hyde, E 1993 'The life and work of Herbert J Rowse'. Unpublished MPhil thesis, Liverpool John Moores University, Appendix: Reminiscences of Rex Brown, 23
Holland, J and Jackson, I 2013 'A monument to humanism: Pilkington Brothers' headquarters (1955–1965) by Fry, Drew and Partners'. *Architectural History* **56**, 2013 343–86

1936
Alterations to Scottish Equitable Assurance
Castle Street, Liverpool

1936
New farm house and alterations to Spurston Hall
Client: Mr R Neilson

1937
Voss Motor Company Showrooms**
Mann Island, Liverpool
A single-storey building of brick with stone dressings, demolished in 2007 as part of the redevelopment of Mann Island with apartments and offices.

1938
King George V Memorial
Liverpool

1938
Synagogue***
Hope Place, Liverpool

1938
United Kingdom Pavilion
Empire Exhibition**
Bellahouston Park, Glasgow
The Liverpolitan **5**/5, May 1936, 7
Architects' Journal **86**, 21 Oct 1937, 611
Architects' Journal **87**, 12 May 1938, 775
Architectural Design & Construction **8**/6, Jun 1938, 213
Architectural Review **113**, Jul 1938, 30, 58
Reilly, C H 1938 'The Glasgow Exhibition: second thoughts', *Manchester Guardian*, 22 Jun 1938, 11
Baxter, J N 1982 'Thomas S Tait and the Glasgow Empire Exhibition 1938'. MA thesis, University of Glasgow
Baxter, J N 1984 'Thomas S Tait and the Glasgow Empire Exhibition 1938'. *Thirties Society Journal*, **4**, 26–30
Crampsey, B 1988 *The Empire Exhibition of 1938: The Last Durbar*. Edinburgh: Mainstream Publishing, 64
Kinchin, P and Kinchin, J 1988 *Glasgow's Great Exhibitions 1888, 1901, 1911, 1938, 1988*. Bicester: White Cockade, 126–67
Hyde, E 1993 'The life and work of Herbert J Rowse'. Unpublished MPhil thesis, Liverpool John Moores University, Appendix: Reminiscences of Rex Brown, 18–20
Crinson, M 2003 *Modern Architecture and the End of Empire*. Aldershot: Ashgate, 92–7

United Kingdom Pavilion, Empire Exhibition, Glasgow

1939
Finnieston Bridge***
Glasgow
The Builder **164**/5233, 21 May 1943, 454
Architects' Journal **97**, 3 Jun 1943, 363
Hyde, E 1993 'The life and work of Herbert J Rowse'. Unpublished MPhil thesis, Liverpool John Moores University, 166–7, 287

1939
Woolston Primary School***
Huyton, Lancashire
Client: Lancashire County Council
Architect & Building News **189**, 3 Jan 1947, 5
The Builder **174**/5493, 28 May 1948, 647
Building abandoned because of the war.

1940–4
Various projects for the War Department

1945
Woodchurch Housing Estate
Birkenhead, Cheshire
'Village green or', *Liverpool Echo*, 14 Apr 1944
'Reilly v Robinson', *Birkenhead News*, 29 Apr 1944
Edelman, M 1944 'Planning post war Britain: the example of Birkenhead'. *Picture Post* **24**/2, 8 Jul 1944, 16–20
'Labour threatens to break political truce', *Birkenhead Advertiser*, 8 Jul 1944
Architects' Journal **100**/2584, 3 Aug 1944, 85–7
'Woodchurch plan revised', *Birkenhead News*, 9 Sep 1944
'Layout for the Woodchurch Estate', *The Builder* **167**/5312, 24 Nov 1944, 408–9
Wolfe, L 1945 *The Reilly Plan*. London: Nicholson & Watson, 9–10
'New plan for Woodchurch', *Liverpool Daily Post*, 3 Mar 1945

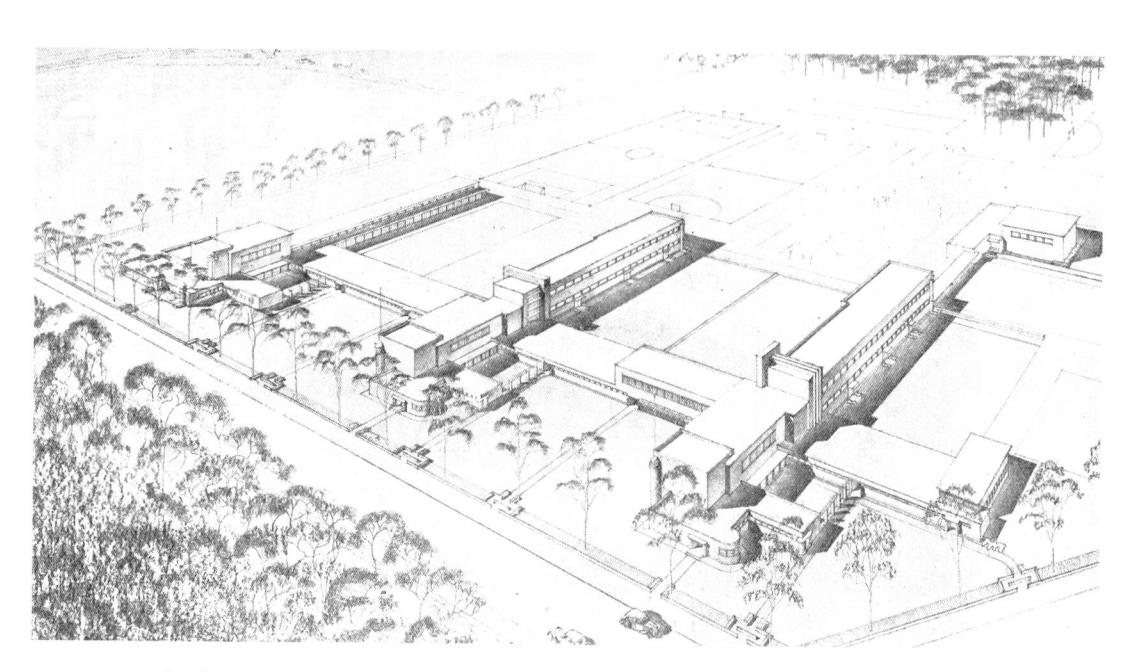

Drawing for Woolston Primary School, Huyton, Lancashire

'Conservatives adopt Rowse plan', *Birkenhead News*, 10 Mar 1945
Architect & Building News **189**, 14 Feb 1947, 132–5; **198**/4269, 13 Oct 1950, 406–10
'Woodchurch Estate', *Building* **25**/10, Oct 1950, 366–70
Architects' Journal **185**/11, 18 Mar 1987, 48–57
Architects' Journal **187**/31, 3 Aug 1988, 33–43
Hyde, E 1993 'The life and work of Herbert J Rowse'. Unpublished MPhil thesis, Liverpool John Moores University, 23–4

1946
Alterations to Brockhole
(19th-century residence converted to a convalescence home)
Windermere, Westmorland (now Cumbria)
Client: Merseyside Hospitals Council

1947
Conversion of stables at Bankfield Hall
Ulverston, Lancashire (now Cumbria)
Client: Merseyside Hospitals Association

1947
Factory at Kirkby★★★
Lancashire
Client: David Tod Ltd

1949
Factory★★
Netherton, Liverpool
Client: Richmond Sausage Company
Crosby Herald, 3 Feb 1983
Hollinghurst, H 2014 *Waterloo, Seaforth and Litherland Through Time*. Stroud: Amberley Publishing

1950
Pelham Bridge★★★
Lincoln
Hyde, E 1993 'The life and work of Herbert J Rowse'. Unpublished MPhil thesis, Liverpool John Moores University, 167, 287

1951
Diplomatic buildings for Delhi and Karachi★★★
Bertram, M 2017 *Room for Diplomacy: The History of Britain's Diplomatic Buildings Overseas 1800–2000*. Salisbury: Spire Books

1952
Alterations at the Adelphi Hotel
Liverpool
Client: Adelphi Hotel

1953–6
Research laboratories
Cleeve Road, Leatherhead, Surrey
Client: British Electrical and Allied Industries Research Association
Electrical Times **126**/3286, 28 Oct 1954, 630
Electrical Journal **153**/3985, 29 Oct 1954, 1357–8
Electrical Review **155**/18, 29 Oct 1954, 682–4
The Engineer **204**/5293, 5 Jul 1957, 12
Journal of the Institution of Electrical Engineers **3**/24, Oct 1957, 540–1

1960
Sundry work for Midland Bank

Further reading

Barker, T C 1977 *The Glassmakers, Pilkington: The Rise of an International Company 1826–1976*. London: Weidenfeld and Nicolson

Bertram, M 2017 *Room for Diplomacy: The History of Britain's Diplomatic Buildings Overseas 1800–2000*. Salisbury: Spire Books

Booker, J 1990 *Temples of Mammon: The Architecture of Banking*. Edinburgh: Edinburgh University Press

Budden, L (ed) 1932 *The Book of the Liverpool School of Architecture*. Liverpool: The University of Liverpool Press and London: Hodder and Stoughton

Cavanagh, T 1997 *Public Sculpture of Liverpool*. Liverpool: Liverpool University Press

Cheeseman, K 1941 'Designing glass for architectural and interior design uses'. *Art and Industry*, Oct 1941, 110–16

Compton, A (ed) 1999 *Edward Carter Preston, 1885–1965: Sculptor, Painter, Medallist*. Liverpool: University of Liverpool Art Collections

Crinson, M 2003 *Modern Architecture and the End of Empire*. Farnham: Ashgate

Crinson, M and Lubbock, J 1994 *Architecture: Art of Profession? Three Hundred Years of Architectural Education in Britain*. Manchester: Manchester University Press

Crouch, C 2002 *Design Culture in Liverpool, 1880–1914: The Origins of the Liverpool School of Architecture*. Liverpool: Liverpool University Press

Dunne, J and Richmond, P 2008 *The World in One School: The History and Influence of the Liverpool School of Architecture 1894–2008*. Liverpool: Liverpool University Press

Falcus, M 1990 *The Blue Funnel Legend: History of the Ocean Steam Ship Company 1865–1973*. Basingstoke: Macmillan

Falgàs, Victor de 1927 *Arte y decoración en España: arquitectura-arte decorativo*. Barcelona: Casellas Moncanut Hnos

Fraser, M and Kerr, J 2007 *Architecture and the 'Special Relationship': The American Influence on Post-War British Architecture*. London: Routledge

Fry, E M 1975 *Autobiographical Sketches*. London: Elek Books

Gilbert, C 1900 'The financial importance of rapid building'. *Engineering Record* **41**, 30 Jun 1900

Gillespie, A K 2011 *Crossing Under the Hudson: The Story of the Holland and Lincoln Tunnels*. Piscataway, NJ: Rutgers University Press

Henley, D and McNulty, M 2009 *The Original Liverpool Sound: The Royal Liverpool Philharmonic Story*. Liverpool: Liverpool University Press

Holland, J and Jackson, I 2013 'A monument to humanism: Pilkington Brothers' headquarters (1955–1965) by Fry, Drew and Partners'. *Architectural History* **56**, Jan 2013, 343–86

Holder, J 1994 'Reflecting change: Pilkington as a patron of modern architecture and design' in Stamp, G, Lever, J and Powers, A (eds) 1994 *Industrial Architecture (Twentieth Century Architecture* special issue 1). London: Twentieth Century Society, Oct 1994, 65–76

Hudson, B (with Boylan, M) 2003 *The School of Pharmacy, University of London: Medicines, Science and Society, 1842–2012*. Cambridge: Elsevier Academic Press

Hughes, Q 1999 *Liverpool: City of Architecture*. Liverpool: The Bluecoat Press

Hyde, E 1993 'The life and work of Herbert J Rowse'. Unpublished MPhil thesis, Liverpool John Moores University

Jackson, R 2011 *Highway under the Hudson: A History of the Holland Tunnel*. New York: New York University Press

McGrath, R 1937 *Glass in Architecture and Decoration*. London: Architectural Press

Mersey Tunnel Joint Committee 1934 *The Story of the Mersey Tunnel Officially Named Queensway*. Liverpool: Charles Birchall

Pilkington Brothers Limited nd *Vitrolite Specifications*. St Helens: Pilkington Brothers Limited

Pinkham, R 1982 'Interview with Sigmund Pollitzer'. *Thirties Society Journal* 2, 5–12

Poole, S J 1995 'A critical analysis of the work of Herbert Tyson Smith, sculptor and designer. Unpublished PhD Thesis, University of Liverpool

Powers, A 1982 'Architectural education in Britain'. Unpublished PhD thesis, University of Cambridge

Reilly, C 1930 'Some younger architects of today: Herbert J Rowse', *Building* **v**, Dec 1930, 524–9

Reilly, C 1924 *Masters of Architecture: McKim, Mead and White*. London: Ernest Benn

Reilly, C 1921 *Some Liverpool Streets and Buildings in 1921*. Liverpool: Liverpool Daily Post and Mercury

Reilly, C 1906 *Portfolio of measured drawings / [by the students of the] School of Architecture, the University of Liverpool, 1906, Vol 1*. Liverpool: University Press of Liverpool; London: Crosby Lockwood

Richmond, P 2001 *Marketing Modernisms: The Architecture and Influence of Charles Reilly*. Liverpool: Liverpool University Press

Smiles, S (ed) 1998 *Going Modern and Being British: Art, Architecture and Design in Devon 1910–1960*. Exeter: Intellect

Sharples, J 2006 *Liverpool*. New Haven, CT and London: Yale University Press

Sharples, J, Powers, A and Shippobottom, M 1996 *Charles Reilly and the Liverpool School of Architecture 1904–1933*. Liverpool: Liverpool University Press

Stamp, G 1989 'Architectural sculpture in Liverpool' in P Curtis (ed) *Patronage and Practice: Sculpture on Merseyside, Liverpool*. London: Tate Gallery

Twomey, S 2014 'From monumental to modern: Martins Bank and Herbert J Rowse'. Unpublished MArch dissertation, University of Liverpool

Willis, C 1995 *Form Follows Finance: Skyscrapers and Skylines in New York and Chicago*. New York: Princeton Architectural Press

Wolfe, L 1945 *The Reilly Plan: A New Way of Life*. London: Nicholson & Watson

Yeomans, D 1998 'The pre-history of the curtain wall'. *Construction History* **14**, 59–82

The Twentieth Century Society

Without the Twentieth Century Society an entire chapter of Britain's recent history was to have been lost. It was alert when others slept. It is still crucial!
SIMON JENKINS, WRITER, HISTORIAN, JOURNALIST

The Twentieth Century Society campaigns for the preservation of architecture and design in Britain from 1914 onwards and is a membership organisation which you are warmly invited to join and support.

The architecture of the twentieth century has shaped our world and must be part of our future; it includes bold, controversial, and often experimental buildings that range from the playful Deco of seaside villas to the Brutalist concrete of London's Hayward Gallery. The Twentieth Century Society produces many publications of its own to increase knowledge and understanding of this exciting range of work. The Twentieth Century Architects series has enabled the Society to extend its reach through partnership, initially with RIBA Publishing and now with Historic England, contributing the contacts and expertise needed to create enjoyable and accessible introductions to the work of architects who deserve more attention. In the process, the books contribute to the work of protecting buildings from demolition or disfigurement.

We propose buildings for listing, advise on restoration and help to find new uses for buildings threatened with demolition. Join the Twentieth Century Society and not only will you help to protect these modern treasures, you will also gain an unrivalled insight, through our magazine, journal and events programme, into the ground-breaking architecture and design that helped to shape the century.

For further details and to join online, see www.c20society.org.uk

CATHERINE CROFT
DIRECTOR

The Society of Architectural Historians of Great Britain

The Society of Architectural Historians of Great Britain (SAHGB) exists to:

> REPRESENT architectural history in the United Kingdom
> INSPIRE a lifelong enjoyment of architectural history for all
> ENGAGE diverse audiences through professional and public programming
> PROMOTE architectural history at all levels in education, research and publishing
> ADVOCATE for an inclusive architectural history for the public benefit

As the principal subject association for architectural history in the United Kingdom and as a registered charity, we promote the discipline of architectural history through advocacy and charitable giving. We advocate for the subject in higher education, heritage and conservation bodies, and museums and galleries. We award grants to support research and publication, and we are the only organisation of our kind in the UK to award a significant number of annual bursaries for postgraduate study. These awards and scholarships are open to all.

As a membership organisation, we provide opportunities for gathering and exchanging knowledge and ideas about architectural history. Our members study the history of architecture and the built environment of all times and places, and we do so from a wide variety of disciplinary perspectives and institutional settings. We organise a diverse programme of events for our membership and the public. We publish and disseminate research and scholarship through our magazine, *The Architectural Historian*, our leading peer-reviewed journal, *Architectural History*, and across a growing number of other media and platforms.

We are proud to support the Twentieth Century Society in the publication of this landmark series, which makes available, to new and old audiences alike, engaging and accessible scholarship on often long-neglected designers and monuments.

For further details and to join online, see www.sahgb.org.uk

Other titles in the series

Ahrends, Burton and Koralek
Kenneth Powell
Apr 2012
978-1-85946-166-2

Aldington, Craig and Collinge
Alan Powers
Nov 2009 *(out of print)*
978-1-85946-302-4

Alison and Peter Smithson
Mark Crinson
Jun 2018
978-1-84802-352-9

Arup Associates
Kenneth Powell
Jun 2018
978-1-84802-367-3

Stephen Dykes Bower
Anthony Symondson
Dec 2011
978-1-85946-398-7

Chamberlin, Powell & Bon
Elain Harwood
Nov 2011
978-1-85694-397-0

Wells Coates
Elizabeth Darling
Jul 2012
978-1-85946-437-3

Frederick Gibberd
Christine Hui Lan Manley
Sep 2017
978-1-84802-273-7

Howell Killick Partridge & Amis
Geraint Franklin
Jun 2017
978-1-84802-275-1

McMorran & Whitby
Edward Denison
Oct 2009
978-1-85946-320-8

John Madin
Alan Clawley
Mar 2011
978-1-85946-367-3

Robert Maguire & Keith Murray
Gerald Adler
Mar 2012
978-1-85946-165-5

Leonard Manasseh & Partners
Timothy Brittain-Catlin
Dec 2010
978-1-85946-368-0

Powell & Moya
Kenneth Powell
Apr 2009
978-1-85946-303-1

Ryder and Yates
Rutter Caroll
Apr 2009
978-1-85946-266-9

Forthcoming titles

Architects' Co-Partnership
Alan Powers
978-1-84802-575-2

Edward Cullinan
Kenneth Powell
978-1-84802-557-8

Ralph Erskine
Elain Harwood
978-1-84802-559-2

Ernö Goldfinger
Elain Harwood and Alan Powers
978-1-84802-274-4

Patrick Gwynne
Neil Bingham
978-1-84802-276-8

Peter Moro
Alistair Fair
978-1-84802-561-5

John Outram
Geraint Franklin
978-1-84802-558-5

Walter Segal
John McKean
978-1-84802-560-8

F X Velarde
Andrew Crompton and Dominic Wilkinson
978-1-84802-548-6

William Whitfield
Roland Jeffery
978-1-84802-573-8

Illustration credits

The author and publisher have made every effort to contact copyright holders and will be happy to correct, in subsequent editions, any errors or omissions that are brought to their attention.

Archimage/Alamy Stock Photo
p 74 (BHKE7N)

Architects' Journal
pp xiii (11 April 1935), 40l and 40r (19 Oct 1932)

Architectural Press Archive/RIBA Collections
pp 110 (RIBA7656), 124 (RIBA15597), 133 (RIBA25868)

Architectural Review
pp 44, 48t, 49l (June 1934)

Barclays Group Archives
pp x, 25, 26, 27l, 27r, 28, 32t, 32b

Birkenhead Library
pp 93, 104, 106t, 106b, 108t

The Book of Liverpool School of Architecture
pp 7, 8, 10, 12, 39t, 39b, 127

Building Journal
p 24 (April 1930)

© Cumbria Archive Service
pp 96, 97

John Davidson/Alamy Stock Photo
p 57l

Tom Harker
pp 22t, 22b

© Elain Harwood
pp 62, 70–71

© Historic England Archive (photographer Alun Bull)
Front cover (DP233633),
pp 42 (DP233729), 57r (DP233630), 58–59 (DP233634), 61r (DP233627)

© Iain Jackson
Frontispiece, pp 9, 36, 37tl, 37t, 51br, 61l, 90, 108b, 113, 128

Liverpool Public Records Office
pp 14, 65t, 65b, 68, 69, 72

Lloyds Archive
pp 18, 21

Martins Bank Archive
pp 4t, 34t, 34b, 129

© National Trust Images/Edward Chambré Hardman Collection
pp 29l (149391), 29r (149118), 48b (149368), 50 (149239)

Courtesy of NSG
pp 77, 78t, 78b, 79, 80, 82

ILLUSTRATION CREDITS

Pharmacy Archive
pp 87, 88

PRISMA ARCHIVO/Alamy Stock Photo
p 35 (MBDNYC)

Private collection
p 104

© RIBA
p 83 (RIBA101045)

© RIBA Collections
p 11 (RIBA135357)

© Royal Liverpool Philharmonic
p 73

Story of the Mersey Tunnel
pp 54b, 54tr, 56, 60

The Builder
pp 6t (22 November 1912), 6b (28 April 1911; Source: Historic England Archive), 15, 16, 17 (October 1923)

Charlie Tomalin/Alamy Stock Photo
p 20

© Towner Images
pp 37b, 49r, 51tl, 51tr, 51bl

University of Liverpool, Special Collections and Archives
pp 4b, 67

By courtesy of The University of Liverpool
pp xvi, 3, 30, 54tl, 55

Unknown Source
Back cover

© Wirral Archives
pp 94, 102, 103

Reproduced with the permission of Wirral Council
p 99

145

Index

Illustrations are indicated by page numbers in **bold**.

Aberconway, Lord 91, 125
Abercrombie, Patrick 53, 75, 100
Aintree (Lancs), Littlewood's Mail Order premises 132
America, construction techniques and influences xi, 2–7, **4**, 19, 20, 27, 31, 33
Amersterdam School vii
Armitage, Revd J J R 53

Bale, Stewart 77
Barcelona (Spain)
  Headquarters building 38, 129, **129**
  International Exhibition 38, 63
Belgium 112
Birkenhead (Wirral)
  Hamilton Square Tunnel 46
  Mersey Tunnel
    entrances 47, **54**
    history 43, 45
    ventilation shafts 57–61, **57**, **58–60**, **61**, 131
  St Andrews Square flats 92–5, **93**, **94**, 132
  Woodchurch estate
    context 95–100, **96–7**, **99**
    Reilly's plan 100–3, **102**, **103**
    Rowse's role 90, 103–9, **104–6**, **108**, 112, 134–5
Bloomfield, Edward 67
Blundellsands (Lancs), conservatory 7, **7**, 125
Bowden (Ches), Levanton 129

Bradshaw, Donald 20–1, 112
Bradshaw, Rowse and Harker 113
brick
  Pharmacy Building 85
  Philharmonic Hall 66–7
  Pilkington's 80–1
  St Andrew's Square 94–5
  Woodchurch 112
  Woodside ventilation tower xiv, 13, **61**, 63, 111
Briggs, Frank Gatley 15
Brittain, T A 109
Brodie, John 43–4, 127
Bromsgrove Guild 19
Budden, Lionel 7, 11, 52, 53, 126
Burton (Ches), St Nicholas Church 112, **113**

Cambridge (Cambs)
  King's College Library 11, 126
  Rowse lecture xiii
Capstick, George 36, 50
Cheeseman, Kenneth 75, 76, 80, 81, 83
Chicago (USA), buildings 27
Childwall (Lancs), Lloyds Bank 38, **39**, 129
Clarke, Denis 91, 98–100
Cockerell, Charles 1, 23
Compania Sud Americana, interior designs 129
concrete xiv, 10
Connell, Sir Robert Lowdon 7, 125

Corbett, Harvey 20
Córdoba (Spain), Palacio de los Villalones 40
Coventry (W Mids), Municipal Buildings 5, **6**, 125
Crabtree, William 75
Cunningham, John 64

Dod, Harold 7, 23
Dudok, Willem Marinus vii, 66

Edelman, Maurice 101
Egan, William 98–100
Elizabeth, the Queen Mother 83
Elmes, Harvey 1
Fitzmaurice, Sir Maurice 43–4
Florence (Italy)
  Palazzo Strozzi 19
  Santa Maria Maggiore 112
Forshaw, John 100
Foster, John Junior 1
Fry, Edwin Maxwell 7

George V 43, 52, 53, 133
George's Dock ventilation tower (Liverpool) 47–9, 130
  decoration xii, 50–2, **50**, **51**
  repairs 112
  section **49**
  views of **x**, **xiii**, **42**, **48**
Glasgow (Glas)
  Finnieston Bridge 134

146

INDEX

Glasgow Empire Exhibition 63, 82, **124**, 133, **133**
Gloag, John 75
Gordon, H J 53
Greenwich Hospital (G London) 2
György, Dénes 38

Harker, Thomas 112
Heswall (Ches)
   Allandale 8–9, **9**, 125
   Garthlands 10, **10**, 126
   Golf Club 11, **11**, 127
   West Hey house 128
Hewett, Bertram 47, 52
Higgins, W W 132
Hilversum (Neths), Town Hall 66
Hodel, Josef A 74
Holden, Charles 84
Holland, Clifford 45
Holt, Alfred & Co 14–15, 19, 31, 126
Horder, Percy Morley 85
Huggill, H P 53
Hughes, John 66, 81, 92
Huyton (Lancs), Woolston primary school 134, **134**
Hyde, Eric xii, 21

India Buildings (Liverpool) 14–21, 126
   aerial view **x**
   arcade ceiling vaults 20
   competition drawings 15–17
   Lloyds Bank interior 21
   old **14**, 15
   repairs 112
   Rowse practice at 21
   rusticated base 18
   trans-Atlantic feel vii

Insulight 75
Jerez (Spain), Los Alamos's house 33, **34**
Johnson, Amy xii
Johnson, T H & Son 75–6

Karachi (Pakistan), Diplomatic buildings 135
Keay, Lancelot 92, 95
Kelly, Sydney 91, 125
Kirby, Edmund 14, 23
Kirk Sandall (S Yorks), hotel 75
Kirkby (Lancs), factory 135

Lansdown & Brown 85
Leatherhead (Surrey), research labs 135
Lever, William Hesketh (Lord Leverhulme) 2, 5, 95
Lincoln (Lincs), Pelham Bridge 135
Linstead, H H 85
Liverpool (Lancs)
   Adelphi Hotel 135
   Castle Street, Scottish Equitable Assurance 132
   Church Street, Lloyds Bank 40–1, **40**, 128, 130
   Civic Design School 2, 5
   Cotton Exchange 5
   Dale Street, Midland Bank 113
   Fire Salvage Association 129
   George V memorial 133
   Great Howard Street, Bibby & Sons 129
   Hope Place, synagogue 133
   housing 91–2
   Manbré and Garton sugar refinery **12**, 13, 125

Mann Island, Voss Motor Co Showrooms 133
Menlove Gardens, house 127
Netherton, Richmond sausage factory 112, 135
St Andrew's Gardens 92
St Paul's Eye Hospital 130
School of Architecture 1–2, 52, 53
Town Hall **25**
see also India Buildings; Martins Bank; Mersey Tunnel; Philharmonic Hall
Liverpool Architectural Society xiii, 38, 52
London
   Bush House 20, 33
   Daily Express building 76
   Peter Jones store 75, 76, 81
   Pharmacy Building 55, 83–9, **83**, **87**, **88**, 132
   Selfridge's 41

McKim, Mead & White 7, 31
MARS group 63
Marshall, J Ernest 7
Martins Bank (Liverpool) 23–36, 128–9
   decoration 33–6, **37**, **128**
   drawings **24**, **27**, **28**
   exterior **x**, **25**, **26**
   influences xi
   interiors **32**, **34**, **36**
   Rowse practice at 21, **22**
   steel frame 27–31, **30**
   under construction **29**, **110**
Martins mobile bank 38, **39**, 129
Mawson, Edward Prentice 95
Mawson, Thomas H 95, 96, 97
Menyhért, Nikolaus 38

Mersey Tunnel (Liverpool/
  Birkenhead) 127
above-ground structures
  47–52, **48**, **56**, **57**
an appreciation vii
free pass 21
history of 43–7, **44**
influences 38
public support and
  opening 52–61, **54**, **55**
Seacombe tower 113
see also Birkenhead, Mersey
  Tunnel; George's Dock
  ventilation tower; New
  Quay ventilation station;
  North John Street
  ventilation tower; Old
  Haymarket tunnel
  entrance; Sidney Street
  ventilation station; Taylor
  Street ventilation station;
  Woodside ventilation
  station
Midland Bank 135
Modernism xiv, 63, 92, 111
Mott, Sir Basil 43–4, 45–6,
  47, 55, 127

Neilson R 132
New Delhi (India), Diplomatic
  buildings 112, 135
New Quay ventilation station
  (Liverpool) 130
New York (USA)
  Holland Tubes 45, 46
  National City Bank 31
North John Street ventilation
  tower (Liverpool) 49, **49**,
  52, 130
Old Haymarket tunnel
  entrance (Liverpool) 52,
  131

Ormskirk (Lancs), York
  Cottage 126, **127**
Owens, Richard & Son 1

Parry, Mr 8, 125
Parry, Dorothy 8
Philharmonic Hall (Liverpool)
  64–74, 131
  exterior **68**
  influences vi, vii–viii
  interior **62**, **69**, 70–2, **73**, **74**
  old 64, **65**
Pilkington, Geoffrey 75
Pittsburgh (USA), Liberty
  Tunnels 46
Pollitzer, Sigmund 75, 79, 80
Port Sunlight (Ches) 2, **4**, 95,
  109
Prentice, Alderman 103
Prestatyn (Denbighs),
  housing estate 5, 91, 125
Preston, Edward Carter 81
  student project **4**, 5
Pritchard, Wood & Partners
  75
Puddington (Ches)
  Chapel House 112
  Puddington Hall and
    cottages 132

Rainhill (Lancs), Hulton
  Avenue estate 91, 125
Rees, Verner O 85
Reilly, Sir Charles Herbert
  Liverpool School of
    Architecture 1–5, 7
  on
    Glasgow Empire Exhibi-
      tion 63, 82
    India Buildings 18
    Lloyds Bank, Castle
      Street 41

  Lloyds Bank, Childwall 38
  Martins Bank 29, 31
  Rainhill housing 91
  patronage xii, 11, 23, 29,
    38, 40, 92, 129
  Woodchurch estate 100–3,
    102, **103**, 104–5, 107
Rice, Alwyn Edward, concert
  hall 66, **67**
Robinson, Bertie 98, 99, 101–2
Rohe, Mies van der 38
Rowse family
  Christopher 112
  Dorothy (née Parry) 8
  Herbert James 1–7, 8, **110**,
    112
  Sarah Ann 8, 126
Ruiz, Hernàn II 40

St Helens (Lancs), Pilkington's
  offices and canteen 55,
  75–83, **77–9**, **80**, **82**, 132
Scarlett, Arthur 20–1, 112
Shaw, Norman 14
Shaw, Thomas 36
Sidney Street ventilation
  station (Birkenhead) 131
Simon, Frank 5
Skeaping, John 66
Spencely and Minoprio 64
Spurston Hall (Ches) 132
steel-framed construction
  xiv, 2–5, 19, 27–31, **30**, 63
Stephenson, Gordon 107

Taylor Street ventilation
  station (Birkenhead) 131
Thompson, Edmund C, work
  by
  India Buildings 19
  Lloyds Bank 40, 130
  Mersey Tunnel 50, 130

Philharmonic Hall 74, **74**
Thornley, Arnold 11, 15, 20, 23, 76, 126
Thornton Hough (Ches), Rocklands 132
Thornton Manor (Merseys) 95
Thurstaston (Ches), house 126
Tod, David, Ltd 135
Town Planning Review 2
Towndrow, Frederic 61
Truscon 95
Tyson Smith, Herbert, work by 35, 40, 130

Ulverston (Cumbria), Bankfield Hall 135

Van Gruisen, Alderman 93
Verona (Italy)
　Palazzo della Gran Guardia **xv**, 2, **3**
　Palazzo Pompeii 2
Vitrolite 75, 76–9, **79**

War Department 134
Whistler, Reginald Hector, glass by **73**, 74, 75
Willaston (Ches), Millmead House 8–9, **8**, 126
Willink, W E 23
Willink & Thicknesse 14
Windermere (Cumbria), Brockhole 135
Winnipeg (Canada), Manitoba Parliament Building xi, 5, **6**
Wolfe, Lawrence 102
Wood, Sir Henry 64
Woodside ventilation station (Birkenhead) 131
Wright, Lawrence 53

Zaragoza (Spain), Aljafería Palace 33, **35**